EARLE BIRNEY

Ghost in the Wheels

SELECTED POEMS

McClelland and Stewart

The Canadian Publishers,
McClelland and Stewart Limited
25 Hollinger Road, Toronto

Manufactured by Webcom Limited

Canadian Cataloguing in Publication Data

Birney, Earle, 1904-
Ghost in the wheels

ISBN 0-7710-1408-2 pa.

I. Title.

PS8503.I7A6 1977   C811'.5'4   C77-001456-9
PR9199.3.B58A6 1977

For Christopher and Earle

Contents

Preface

People who just want to enjoy what follows should skip this preface. It's for "students" and "teachers", though of little use to them either, since I'm talking only about origins, how a few of these things came about. Autobiographical gossip. And I should like to say at the start that I don't any longer like the words "poet", "poems", etc. They've developed pretentious connotations. I prefer "maker" and "makings". They mean the same but the texture's plainer, oatmeal, not manna.

A high school girl comes up after a reading. Did it really happen to you? Were you engaged to a girl with violet eyes? (Yes, but only when she wore a violet dress). . . . Or an undergrad engineer wants to know how my Lake Opal can be both in the High Rockies and close to Vancouver. (It's my prototype lake.) Where's that? (In the Big Rock Candy Mountains.) The distrust in his eyes darkens to conviction: I am a geographical moron. . . . The Canadian approach to "poetry" is often more literal than literate. I wrote a book to disprove, among other legends, the belief that I did push my best friend off a cliff.* But there are students, and at best one "professor of Can. Lit.", who still doubt my word. After all, I once climbed mountains, and I told "David" in the first person, didn't I?

The colonial past, still with us, inclines us to think that real invention takes place only elsewhere. Apart from Alexander Graham Bell and Stephen Leacock, well, who *was* there? When the new novelists write about what they know, the reviewers still hunt for self-confession, as they did in my day. I was once a radical and later a soldier; the anti-heroes of my two novels have therefore to be me.

As for my makings—if I didn't actually try on everything for size in an Australian Museum of Man, why do I say I would? Readers for whom science is science fiction, and astronomy astrology, will find everything a documentary, and humour an irrelevancy. Verses, in particular, may be thought of as only fragments from a diary, prettied up, except for real Lyrics like in Rock. But I have no absolutes, and can "explain" my own stuff only by setting off in a relative way, like the chap in the Einsteinian limerick, who returned the previous night. I start a making out of a yen to set down a momentary insight, a temporary "truth" relating somehow to me. But what turns out is always different, either because the perception got blurred putting it down, or luckily got sharper, ranging beyond the "reality" that triggered it and rumbling into a sort of dance with words.

---

* *The Cow Jumped over the Moon,* a would-be textbook on the writing and reading of poetry, Toronto, 1972. It was universally rejected by the Canadian educational systems, and is obtainable only from the author.

I am taking a snap of a Thailand canal from a bridge one afternoon when a tiny naked boy runs in front of my camera. A man, presumably the boy's father, solicitous of the tourist, scolds him. I fumble up a coin and a bit of chocolate for him, the father smiles, the little one leaps from tears with a spontaneous dance of delight. I have a flash of identification with him that cuts through the veils of language, cultures, age. Later, writing it down, I become aware of many overtones, ironic, even pathetic. Earlier that day I'd seen bodies being dumped on the steps of a dying-house—cholera epidemic—and I'd walked on, the untouchable tourist, to view the gold-leafed temple-tombs and return for a swim at my American hotel to the sound of a jazz band. The night before I'd spent partly in talk with smokers in an opium establishment, partly watching a chorus of Hong Kong girls strip on a Bangkok stage. So this making grew from a moppet's jig to embrace my fear of guilty indifference to the human condition. Perhaps. At this moment I see it this way.

"Meeting of strangers" is a documentary—almost. Yes, I did get off a ship in Port-of-Spain and foolishly begin walking alone at dusk through the apparently deserted dockside. Yes, I will swear it (but there are no witnesses), I was nearly knifed and robbed of a six-dollar jacket. But I was white, and so looked prosperous. Colour me rich, colour him poor. And a taxi happened along, like a scene in a bad movie, and my thug shouted something I couldn't hear as I rolled away. But the driver couldn't either. So the last line, without which this piece would be only a fragment of travel-diary, had to be invented. The poem requires that jeering send-off, whatever he "really" said. Life presented me with a serio-comic puzzle and left out the key piece. I had to make one fit, in the interests of a different truth. It had to be a *Selbst-Ironie*, a self-mockery, for I was the fool of this scene.

The case of "Twenty-third flight" was similar. Here you could say every line to the last was true. A beautiful girl greeter was waiting at the steps of the plane to garland and buss me when I arrived, an aging green-horn, in the Honolulu airport. She was from a luxury hotel and I was her only passenger, a fraud, a one-night splurger, flush for the moment on Lord Nuffield's charity to scholars. So there was a ritual, a contemporary fantasy, we had to conduct together. To make the piece, no details needed invention—only a style had to be found, to bring it all down from the commercially solemn to the mock-heroic, where again I must rightly play the fool. What classical voice should I borrow? I remembered my Flight Number (23), invoked the voice of King David, or rather King James's Committee, and at once the details of "reality" selected and ordered themselves into what I hope to be comedy.

Some youthful readers have expressed surprise, however, and some middle-aged ones disapproved, when they realized the Me of that making was actually fifty-four, and the one in "Curaçao" fifty-eight. Of course. This is the point of it. I am my own clown. Read Yeats's "Tower". So often it's the would-be critic who can't stand reality. Inside every healthy ancient is a trapped youth still lusting.

Sometimes the energy to spark a piece lies hidden till the last moment. One spring day in 1964 a friend and I came for the first time to Epidaurus. As we climbed the steps of the world's oldest theatre, I was trying to imagine what it was like to be part of an audience there for, say, a Sophocles opening 2500 years ago. It would have been a raw new theatre then, whose erecting no doubt destroyed the peace of the fashionable resthome by the hot springs. But that hotel had been in turn a vulgarizing, an intrusion on an Aesculapian temple. If I knew more Greek history, I thought, I would try to make something—especially as I found, looking again in my guidebook, that the temple too was an invasion of the holiness of a primitive well. And now I am one of the two Canadians creating our own sacrilege, with the assistance of an unavoidable Greek guide. He has placed himself in the exact stone centre of the repaired *orkestra* and is waiting till we reach the top row and listen. Then he will drop the small pin he holds. . . . He does, and we hear it, sharing with all the audiences back to Sophocles the marvel of classical acoustics. But all this isn't demanding a making from me. Something else is nagging, more ominous, not at all nostalgic.

Just before the pin dropped I remembered that a half-hour ago the guide had asked me in careful English if it were true, as his morning paper had headlined, that Soviet China had just made and set off a hydrogen bomb. He now, down at the amphitheatre's eye, we on the rim, have ears cocked for another pin.

If any of all this seems dogmatic, not put in a relative way, it's only my clumsiness. I suspect I've said nothing about "poetry" that's more than half-right. About all I can be sure about is that there are some eighty-six makings in this book, none I think great and none I hope bad. They are supposed to be in chronological order of the first draftings—but it's hard to remember. Anything missing here and not in the *Collected Poems* is either sunk without trace or floating about waiting for a boat.

Earle Birney
June 1977

ONCE HIGH UPON A HILL

Up was down   was up   enchanted   & still is
or else to look back so far is to escape all gravities

Undergrad inseparables 4 years before in Canada
long bony me   longer bonier Slim
trails joined again haphazard here
on what a camping ground!   the Pacific's only City
(LA? actors & football colleges)   San Francisco   SF
(men of the world now   we never called it Frisco)
Our tent a 20$ furnished shack complete with fleas
propped on a gusty ledge of hill   no no   *the* Hill
(nostalgia overcomes me)   *Telegraph*   in 1930
before rich ladies conquered it with phallic towers

Stone eyes of Giulio's goat   the weird joy
that first morning in our wobbly hideout
(revolving now some 15,000 light-mornings under/over)
to see them glaring down from that primeval rockcave
old Giulio from Sardinia had built into his cellar
Down was up & sidewise & every map Italian
I'd prised the one window open to smell Freedom
Bohemia   our secret Latin Quarter
but what filtered through the dockweed demonstration
occupying the sheeptrack we had for lane
was purest ramstink   It punched me stumbling
through all the 6-yard length of our new Home
to the back porch   a broomcloset on stilts
where Slim's long nose was sniffing too   grape mash
steaming straight up from someone's blissful lilybed

It's taken some forty years for me to know which smells
& frenzies last: the sound of laughter's with them
though only Slim knows if that's what he hears now
For me the happy waves surprise   fade in on any station
or else I'd give up tuning in at all

Slim & I
go to Telegraph Hill
the Italian section
in San Fran.

New home—rough
& stinks from
a winery

I have to think hard what my worries were
tremendous surely for us both at 25   bad as now
Slim freshly jilted & dropped from a newspaper back home
his novels   my poems   lost somewhere on that virgin moon
Slim selling pickles in SF   me Remedial English in UCal
(both mainly to non-buyers)   o yes I'd flunked the Phoo Dee
for thoughts about Eng. Lit. not in the lectures
In 2 months I'd be a jobless foreigner
Something had started the papers called Recession? Depression?
& me engaged to Susie   fellowslave & holdout for a wedding
Yes   & all that hasnt left me one good stink for savouring

It was Old Berkeley   true   the air still innocent
of crude oil oratory or tear gas   Beside uptight Philology
a clean brook ran through woods (long since murdered)
where the few rebels walked   & Susie met me with a lunch
Sweet potato & eucalyptus   sick smells of academia
its boardinghouses & its sweatshops & fake scholars
Escape was on the Hill   Hell the bloody themes
could be marked in SF & ferried back to Berkeley (they were)
Meantime Susie   violet-eyed & fabulous   would wait of course

Lucky devils   it seemed we had it all   updown & sideways
or would have   once we achieved Sicilian mistresses
mastered Italian   made pals with the real citizens
those blackhanded stevedores from Naples   & Giulio . . .
Somehow only the mothers handled English
Used it when they collected rent or laundry   Except Maria
of the Lilies   who decided we were friends not Feds
& sold us something even she called Dago Red   *wine* (handwritten margin note)
four bits a gallon   you bringa you owna crock
It was our only breakthru   Funeral & shrill as crows
each morning over their tubs between the backyard ledges
Maria's blackskirt sisters cawed a secret language
while they swabbed & slapped & tore & patched the shirts
of all us dirty atheist *inglesi* who imagined
they could seduce their clean Catholic daughters
God knows we tried

Rejected, fucked only academically   selfunbelieving writers
whose aging mothers back home needed cash & careers from us
wernt we downcast as well as uptight   bewitched & buggered?
Is that how you recall us   my old/young fellow-batch?
I doubt it   We cast our balances from different figures
but the column stands   elysian on the Hill
If not   no matter   since nothing does but when it's there
& beatitude alive's too fast for savouring   it's drunk like water
Yet I would stake what's left of mine
your seesaw joy still spins   whatever length of telescope you try

Italians no   but maybe we could pass for artists
poets at least   We changed at evening to scarves
& climbed the crazy staircase-streets to Merto's
the only allnight blindpig on Telegraph
to sip the one beer we could afford
ignored by Billies banged or bearded & never seeing Merto
(turned out she was in Folsom on a legging rap)
Weekday mornings of course the world beheld us
falling headlong to the Embarcadero trams
Slim in his suit   for pickles   haymow hair slicked down
me spectacled & sweatered for the Berkeley ferry
(the already graying Bay   the still blue sky)
dangling yet more bundles of Basic Undergrad
margins bloodstained with my aborted lyrics

Ah but every helterskelter weekday we ended
crabwise on our Roman hideout   where proud as prentice guides
we clung somehow to our only City's only Matterhorn
Pharisees who knew not those on SF's other hills
hills trapped with streets   that blundered slapbang
over the cones of resurrected Francis
squealing with rollercoaster autos & trailing rails
for cable cars stuffed with their compromising tourists
On Telegraph Hill we had no streets   what's more no telegraph
no English   no rich   no cobbles   no cement
Humanists we moved in a sweet haze of deprivation
across the windstink on our blustering seacliff
No wheels at all   not even bikes   only the feet of cavemen
falling down a ladder jungle

[handwritten margin notes, top right:] Mothers at home in Canada expecting more from their sons — Sons happy & feeling successful — It's how you look at success.

[handwritten margin note, left:] of the relatives in the monastery movement where it are...

[handwritten margin notes, right:] relaxation, putting on airs with limited income

[handwritten margin note:] Slim selling pickles

[handwritten margin note:] Off to university

[handwritten, over "elysian":] Paradise

& overhanding up again by wood lianas
to fire & sleep in doubly-blind stone alleys
It was what we'd grown souls for
this union with the last Hopi on a cliff
a Wop Cliff at that   long floated out from Genoa
& grounded like a wobbly hinge beside the Golden Gate
Come to think of it we never missed the Bridges
the Gate's own Self was there the way Drake saw it
the Bay open   to the Philippines
& latenight ferries served as well for us
as for the suicides we never thought of joining
—no boast in that   except of luck
Maverick fleas   too wild & fond of others' blood
(like those forever in our spavined beds)
to bite ourselves   we were busy riding the backs
of all our wooden centipedes jackknifing us plumb down
to separate jails at morning's 8   & up again to Life
at sundown   whatever Life is   when capitalized
Something that whirls at least   however senseless
The moment transient as smoke   yet tall in dreams
as when a great tree or steeple catches fire

It wasn't that we did a thing worth memorandum
failed to build Twat's Tower   or found the City Lights
If all on that Hill were still alive today
not one could recollect us   well Merto maybe
Merto the Great who came back at last
a gullvoiced gaunt Elizabeth the First   Virgin Hill Queen
hip & trippy 30 years too soon
She fell for Slim & bid us to her welcome-home *festeggiare*
We'd made it   Billies of the Hill now & till death do us

A week more & our shack was empty
I had a job in Salt Lake   Susie to join me in the fall
Slim meanwhile moving to her boardinghouse in Berkeley
We'd had a mere 3 months   a something   but no Eden
I think we refused to notice that we'd left it
As if needing some last symbolic gesture of betrayal
we held our final blowout   SusieSlim&I at the snooty Mark
on the last bloodmoney from my UC galleymasters

Or did we?   am I maundering now   of other girls timespaces *(Can't remember exactly what happened)*
It's possible   Imagination makes numerals or Venus
from the seafoam   art's not the only way to simplify the past
senility will do   or plain laziness
I tell it so far as memory's concerned
& memory's now the only one concerned
a destructive child   breaking up *tabulae* for toys
There's some things we forget to keep in mind   *- only remember what you want to.*
& others we are mindful to forget
In the end we never bear to face the truth that nothing's done
that matters   unless it opens to the butterfly
the caterpillar planned   & even that's a thing of one-day matter

The biggest stars they say lack density
but some of them spin brightest in the lens
I'd call that Hill a crazy set we wandered into   *Had a great time but none of it important - experiences of youth*
& mimed our way along the scenic edge
juggling apprehensions & misapprehensions
playing kids   fools   vintage Beats   false
citizens   real lovers
in a comical-historical-pastoral goatplay called Cloudcuckooland   *? ?*
while all the showplace shot toward Centaurus   *a southern constellation*

At least we had no time to invent our parts
try hero roles we could be still regretting
No doubt that growing old is feeling grateful
imaginary land of plenty for the disasters chosen   not even visible
as scars now   except perhaps to others
Cockaignes recalled help me keep going
skindivers rise to dive again
Somewhere in my brain pan   that Hill stands
& turns me on   we wind again our long legs with the hollyhocks
the funstairs the housestilts the geraniums   & hold on
thinking we help to keep the crooked chimneys up
Perhaps we did   until a brokers' generation came to topple them
It could be we brought Arcadia just the extra weight   *They feel lucky they clove the past they did - but that was only accidental*
that stopped the whole ramshack kaboodle from collapsing
in a cloud of sawdust goatshit grapeskins

Today the Hill still inspires in old age - great memories

Or say St. Francis   on his last American cliff
suspended gravity & time   while mortal & imperilled
we leaned *sans souci* down to love our falling likeness
in that fresh blue upside sky   & then we fell

Or did we?   & which way up?
A somersault perhaps   for I'd almost forgotten
it was Slim who stayed   who married Susie
I should ask you both   how you recall it
Was it like that at all?   or cant you hear me
& this is all a letter to the dead?   you don't remember?
No matter   whatever was   our ferris wheel went round
with gusto   its motion made a tune   a living one
allegro   not death's   his rigadoon wont sound
till all that turning stops   & we are neither sideways
up nor blissful down   but free   for all   or nothing

San Francisco 1930/Galiano Island, B.C. 1970

**MAMMORIAL STUNZAS FOR
AIMEE SIMPLE McFARCIN***

                         up
                  end
Ah but I saw her asc

                  upping breeze
         end
in the ass
There was a cloud
                  fall of kew
                         pids
their glostening buttums twankling
in the gaggle-eyed and (deleted) air

We had snuk away from the Stemple
          a   o
the whoop   lo   yah mongrelation
pigging their dolour
bills to the Kliebright wires
We wondered at dawn
                            into the coca-
cold desert
               t
where bitchy   o   souls of cacteyes
              r
prinked at us
Then soddenly she was   gone
with cupidities   vamoostered
with pink angelinoes   O
mamomma we never forguess you
never your bag bloo sheikelgetting Ayes
loused   lost   from allhallow
Hollowood O
Aimee
Aimee
Tekel
Upharsin

Berkeley, California 1931/Montréal 1945

* Aimee Semple Macpherson, b. Ingersoll, Ont., 1890, d. Los Angeles, Calif., 1944.

Has a love fantasy with Amie McFarin - French dialect?

our ship seems reefed
and only the land comes swimming past alaska pass

the firs tramp through the green crescen to the foRE/
downwards fog in DO

SHore'S pIeD coMmotion of
bristled
ROCKS
d r i f t
and blanching

uP from a spew of sPlinters & BaRK A Logchute arrows

(one mark of few that men have scribbled
on this lucky palimpsest of ranges)

at times a shake-built shack exchanges
passive stares with Come & Gone
or eyeless waits with stoven side
to slide its bones in a green tide

age alaska passage alaska passage alaska passage alas-ka pass

Alberni Canal 1934/1947/1960

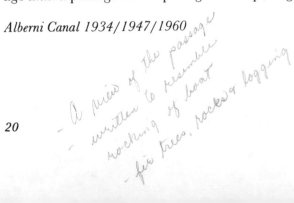

- A piece of the passage
written to resemble
rocking of boat
- fir trees, rocks & logging

DAVID

I

David and I that summer cut trails on the Survey.
All week in the valley for wages, in air that was steeped
In the wail of mosquitoes, but over the sunalive week-ends
We climbed, to get from the ruck of the camp, the surly

Poker, the wrangling, the snoring under the fetid
Tents, and because we had joy in our lengthening coltish
Muscles, and mountains for David were made to see over,
Stairs from the valleys and steps to the sun's retreats.

II

Our first was Mount Gleam. We hiked in the long afternoon
To a curling lake and lost the lure of the faceted
Cone in the swell of its sprawling shoulders. Past
The inlet we grilled our bacon, the strips festooned

On a poplar prong, in the hurrying slant of the sunset.
Then the two of us rolled in the blanket while round us the cold
Pines thrust at the stars. The dawn was a floating
Of mists till we reached to the slopes above timber, and won

To snow like fire in the sunlight. The peak was upthrust
Like a fist in a frozen ocean of rock that swirled
Into valleys the moon could be rolled in. Remotely unfurling
Eastward the alien prairie glittered. Down through the dusty

Skree on the west we descended, and David showed me
How to use the give of shale for giant incredible
Strides. I remember, before the larches' edge,
That I jumped a long green surf of juniper flowing

Away from the wind, and landed in gentian and saxifrage
Spilled on the moss. Then the darkening firs
And the sudden whirring of water that knifed down a fern-hidden
Cliff and splashed unseen into mist in the shadows.

III

One Sunday on Rampart's arête a rainsquall caught us,
And passed, and we clung by our blueing fingers and bootnails
An endless hour in the sun, not daring to move
Till the ice had steamed from the slate. And David taught me

How time on a knife-edge can pass with the guessing of fragments
Remembered from poets, the naming of strata beside one,
And matching of stories from schooldays. . . . We crawled astride
The peak to feast on the marching ranges flagged

By the fading shreds of the shattered stormcloud. Lingering
There it was David who spied to the south, remote,
And unmapped, a sunlit spire on Sawback, an overhang
Crooked like a talon. David named it the Finger.

That day we chanced on the skull and the splayed white ribs
Of a mountain goat underneath a cliff-face, caught
On a rock. Around were the silken feathers of hawks.
And that was the first I knew that a goat could slip.

IV

And then Inglismaldie. Now I remember only
The long ascent of the lonely valley, the live
Pine spirally scarred by lightning, the slicing pipe
Of invisible pika, and great prints, by the lowest

Snow, of a grizzly. There it was too that David
Taught me to read the scroll of coral in limestone
And the beetle-seal in the shale of ghostly trilobites,
Letters delivered to man from the Cambrian waves.

[handwritten margin notes:] Caught in a rainy storm · Chat · clue to impending dangers · David's inexperience

22

V

On Sundance we tried from the col and the going was hard.
The air howled from our feet to the smudged rocks
And the papery lake below. At an outthrust we baulked
Till David clung with his left to a dint in the scarp,

Lobbed the iceaxe over the rocky lip,
Slipped from his holds and hung by the quivering pick,
Twisted his long legs up into space and kicked
To the crest. Then grinning, he reached with his freckled wrist

And drew me up after. We set a new time for that climb.
That day returning we found a robin gyrating
In grass, wing-broken. I caught it to tame but David
Took and killed it, and said, "Could you teach it to fly?"

VI

In August, the second attempt, we ascended The Fortress,
By the forks of the Spray we caught five trout and fried them
Over a balsam fire. The woods were alive
With the vaulting of mule-deer and drenched with clouds all the
morning,

Till we burst at noon to the flashing and floating round
Of the peaks. Coming down we picked in our hats the bright
And sunhot raspberries, eating them under a mighty
Spruce, while a marten moving like quicksilver scouted us.

Bird: symbol of life
damaged life
must die if it
no good if it can't fly

eating off the land.

VII

But always we talked of the Finger on Sawback, unknown
And hooked, till the first afternoon in September we slogged
Through the musky woods, past a swamp that quivered with frog-
    song,
And camped by a bottle-green lake. But under the cold

Breath of the glacier sleep would not come, the moon-light
Etching the Finger. We rose and trod past the feathery
Larch, while the stars went out, and the quiet heather
Flushed, and the skyline pulsed with the surging bloom

Of incredible dawn in the Rockies. David spotted
Bighorns across the moraine and sent them leaping
With yodels the ramparts redoubled and rolled to the peaks,
And the peaks to the sun. The ice in the morning thaw

Was a gurgling world of crystal and cold blue chasms,
And seracs that shone like frozen saltgreen waves.
At the base of the Finger we tried once and failed. Then David
Edged to the west and discovered the chimney; the last

Hundred feet we fought the rock and shouldered and kneed
Our way for an hour and made it. Unroping we formed
A cairn on the rotting tip. Then I turned to look north
At the glistening wedge of giant Assiniboine, heedless

Of handhold. And one foot gave. I swayed and shouted.
David turned sharp and reached out his arm and steadied me,
Turning again with a grin and his lips ready
To jest. But the strain crumbled his foothold. Without

A gasp he was gone. I froze to the sound of grating
Edge-nails and fingers, the slither of stones, the lone
Second of silence, the nightmare thud. Then only
The wind and the muted beat of unknowing cascades.

VIII

Somehow I worked down the fifty impossible feet
To the ledge, calling and getting no answer but echoes
Released in the cirque, and trying not to reflect
What an answer would mean. He lay still, with his lean

Young face upturned and strangely unmarred, but his legs
Splayed beneath him, beside the final drop,
Six hundred feet sheer to the ice. My throat stopped
When I reached him, for he was alive. He opened his gray

legs broken

Straight eyes and brokenly murmured "over . . . over."
And I, feeling beneath him a cruel fang
Of the ledge thrust in his back, but not understanding,
Mumbled stupidly, "Best not to move," and spoke

Of his pain. But he said, "I can't move . . . If only I felt
Some pain." Then my shame stung the tears to my eyes
As I crouched, and I cursed myself, but he cried,
Louder, "No, Bobbie! Don't ever blame yourself.

David asks to be pushed over

I didn't test my foothold." He shut the lids
Of his eyes to the stare of the sky, while I moistened his lips
From our water flask and tearing my shirt into strips
I swabbed the shredded hands. But the blood slid

From his side and stained the stone and the thirsting lichens,
And yet I dared not lift him up from the gore
Of the rock. Then he whispered, "Bob, I want to go over!"
This time I knew what he meant and I grasped for a lie

body is smashed

And said, "I'll be back here by midnight with ropes
And men from the camp and we'll cradle you out." But I knew
That the day and the night must pass and the cold dews
Of another morning before such men unknowing

offer to go for help

The ways of mountains could win to the chimney's top.
And then, how long? And he knew . . . and the hell of hours
After that, if he lived till we came, roping him out.
But I curled beside him and whispered, "The bleeding will stop.

- can't leave him

25

You can last." He said only, "Perhaps . . . For what? A wheelchair,
Bob?" His eyes brightening with fever upbraided me.
I could not look at him more and said, "Then I'll stay
With you." But he did not speak, for the clouding fever.

I lay dazed and stared at the long valley,
The glistening hair of a creek on the rug stretched
By the firs, while the sun leaned round and flooded the ledge,
The moss, and David still as a broken doll.

I hunched to my knees to leave, but he called and his voice
Now was sharpened with fear. "For Christ's sake push me over!
If I could move . . . Or die. . . . " The sweat ran from his forehead,
But only his eyes moved. A hawk was buoying

Blackly its wings over the wrinkled ice.
The purr of a waterfall rose and sank with the wind.
Above us climbed the last joint of the Finger
Beckoning bleakly the wide indifferent sky.

Even then in the sun it grew cold lying there. . . . And I knew
He had tested his holds. It was I who had not. . . . I looked
At the blood on the ledge, and the far valley. I looked
At last in his eyes. He breathed, "I'd do it for you, Bob."

IX

I will not remember how nor why I could twist
Up the wind-devilled peak, and down through the chimney's empty
Horror, and over the traverse alone. I remember
Only the pounding fear I would stumble on It

When I came to the grave-cold maw of the bergschrund . . . reeling
Over the sun-cankered snowbridge, shying the caves
In the névé . . . the fear, and the need to make sure It was there
On the ice, the running and falling and running, leaping

26

Of gaping greenthroated crevasses, alone and pursued
By the Finger's lengthening shadow. At last through the fanged
And blinding seracs I slid to the milky wrangling
Falls at the glacier's snout, through the rocks piled huge

On the humped moraine, and into the spectral larches,
Alone. By the glooming lake I sank and chilled
My mouth but I could not rest and stumbled still
To the valley, losing my way in the ragged marsh.

I was glad of the mire that covered the stains, on my ripped
Boots, of his blood, but panic was on me, the reek
Of the bog, the purple glimmer of toadstools obscene
In the twilight. I staggered clear to a firewaste, tripped

And fell with a shriek on my shoulder. It somehow eased
My heart to know I was hurt, but I did not faint
And I could not stop while over me hung the range
Of the Sawback. In blackness I searched for the trail by the creek

And found it. . . . My feet squelched a slug and horror
Rose again in my nostrils. I hurled myself
Down the path. In the woods behind some animal yelped.
Then I saw the glimmer of tents and babbled my story.

I said that he fell straight to the ice where they found him,
And none but the sun and incurious clouds have lingered
Around the marks of that day on the ledge of the Finger,
That day, the last of my youth, on the last of our mountains.

Toronto 1940

VANCOUVER LIGHTS

About me the night   moonless   wimples the mountains
wraps ocean   land   air   and mounting
sucks at the stars   The city   throbbing below
webs the sable peninsula   The golden
strands overleap the seajet   by bridge and buoy
vault the shears of the inlet   climb the woods
toward me   falter   and halt   Across to the firefly
haze of a ship on the gulf's erased horizon
roll the lambent spokes of a lighthouse

Through the feckless years we have come to the time
when to look on this quilt of lamps is a troubling delight
Welling from Europe's bog   through Africa flowing
and Asia   drowning the lonely lumes on the oceans
tiding up over Halifax   now to this winking
outpost comes flooding the primal ink

On this mountain's brutish forehead with terror of space
I stir   of the changeless night and the stark ranges
of nothing   pulsing down from beyond and between
the fragile planets   We are a spark beleaguered
by darkness   this twinkle we make in a corner of emptiness
how shall we utter our fear that the black Experimentress
will never in the range of her microscope find it?   Our Phoebus
himself is a bubble that dries on Her slide   while the Nubian
wears for an evening's whim a necklace of nebulae

Yet we must speak   we the unique glowworms
Out of the waters and rocks of our little world
we conjured these flames   hooped these sparks
by our will   From blankness and cold we fashioned stars
to our size   and signalled Aldebaran
This must we say   whoever may be to hear us
if murk devour   and none weave again in gossamer:

handwritten annotations:
Looking at city - its harbours mountains bridges etc.

Ships from everywhere

We are insignificant - just a twinkle of light

red star in eye of Tauras
- brightest star in Hyades

'a film of cobwebs floating in air in calm weather
- light, delicate, tenuous

                              These rays were ours
we made and unmade them   Not the shudder of continents
doused us   the moon's passion   nor crash of comets
In the fathomless heat of our dwarfdom   our dream's combustion
we contrived the power   the blast that snuffed us
No one bound Prometheus   Himself he chained
and consumed his own bright liver   O stranger
Plutonian   descendant   or beast in the stretching night—
there was light

1941

We are significant even if we are only a small light in the magnificence of the Universe.

WAR WINTERS

process of changing pig iron to steel.

Sun
proud Bessemer   peltwarmer beauty
these winters yoke us   We scan sky for you
The dun droppings blur   we drown in snow
Is this tarnished chimneyplug   in a tenantless room
this sucked wafer   white simpleton
you?

Not
chiefly the months   mould you heartcharmer
to scant hammerdent   on hardiron sky
not alone latitude   to lodgers on this
your slantwhirling lackey   lifecrusted satellite
this your own wrynecked   woedealing
world

not all the Sun's fault – winter so harsh?

Hazelton Avenue, Toronto 1941

damning the sun

THE ROAD TO NIJMEGEN*
(for gabrielle)

December my dear on the road to Nijmegen
between the stones and the bitten sky
was your face

Not yours at first
but only the countenance of lank canals
and gathered stares
(too rapt to note my passing)
of graves with frosted billy-tins for epitaphs
bones of tanks beside the stoven bridges

and old men in the mist
hacking the last chips
from a boulevard of stumps

These for miles and the fangs of homes
where women wheeled in the wind
on the tireless rims of their cycles
like tattered sailboats,
tossing over the cobbles

and the children
groping in gravel for knobs of coal
or clustered like wintered flies
at the back of messhuts
their legs standing like dead stems out of their clogs

Numbed on the long road to mangled Nijmegen
I thought that only the living of others assures us
the gentle and true we remember as trees walking
Their arms reach down from the light of kindness
into this Lazarus tomb

Handwritten margin notes:
Dreams of Gabrielle among graves
men searching for warmth
women
& starving children search for fuel
only thoughts of the living make this bearable

So peering through sleet as we neared Nijmegen
I glimpsed the rainbow arch of your eyes
Over the clank of the jeep
your quick grave laughter
outrising at last the rockets
brought me what spells I repeat
as I travel this road
that arrives at no future
and what creed I can bring
to our daily crimes
to this guilt
in the griefs of the old
and the graves of the young

*Nijmegen was in 1944-45 the town at the tip of the Canadian salient in Holland, connected with rearward troops by a single much-bombed highway. The area had been the scene of tank battles, artillery duels, air raids, buzz-bomb and V-2 rocket attacks. It had also been denuded of trees, coal and foodstocks by the retreating Germans. The winter was in all Europe one of the coldest of the century.

THIS PAGE MY PIGEON
(for esther)

This page is my pigeon sailing
out of the blasted Now to you
my greenest past   my rivered future
See   round his leg snug   love's cylinder

come from this world of wild undoing
from all this quarrel of iron and growth
Weaving by snake-spit of ack-ack and robot's
roar-horror   up past the beautiful brutal

bombers floating like flakes of mica
leaps my faithful feathered one   soars
through the haired and dirty clouds of the war
cleaving cleanly the selfcentered sky

Under apathetic suns and over
the pointless ocean he arrows   off
to the one unlosable loft
What does he say for me   what brings my homer?

Says that your voice still waters my memory
your eyes are leads to the wide light
that will be   Swears you are part of the rightness
of hills   the saneness of music and hemlocks

Says the giraffish dockweed   loneliness
was lopped away long ago   burned in your vaulting fire
when first you gardened me   Now this gyring
windstorm of absence whirls ashes up only

Windseed is barren   takes no truehold
in heart tendrilled tight with existence of you

Portsmouth 1944

LooN about to laugh

– A loon is the only one who would laugh in time of war – 1944.

England 1944/Vancouver 1970

loon: idler, lout
– mistress, harlot
– boy
– a crazy person
– simpleton

YOUNG VETERANS

They return with new cells, old eyes
to their strange children and older wives
They try to be as they were remembered
or to contrive how they are rendered
and failing are themselves again. . . .

Memory of deeds and of their causes
rusts with the capbadge in the closet
Hates like souvenirs are thumbed awhile
then lost in moving or by the playing child. . . .

The soldiers merge and move with all of us
toward whatever mystery
bemused that fatal pliant fish
who first forgot the sea

Christie Military Hospital, Toronto 1945

[handwritten margin note: changes made by war / war forgotten or set aside as life goes on]

MAPPEMOUNDE
(for margaret)

No not this old   whalehall can whelm us
shiptamed gullgraced   soft to our glidings
Harrows that mere more   which squares our map
See in its north   where scribe has marked *mermen*
shore-sneakers who croon   to the seafarer's girl
next year's gleewords   East and west *nadders*
flamefanged bale-twisters   their breath dries up tears
chars in the breast-hoard   the brave picture-faces
Southward *Cetegrande* that   sly beast who sucks in
with whirlwind also   the wanderer's pledges
That sea is hight Time   it hems all hearts' landtrace
Men say the redeless   reaching its bounds
topple in maelstrom   tread back never
Adread in that mere   we drift to map's end

Hospital Ship El Nil, *Atlantic 1945*

ATLANTIC DOOR

Through or over the deathless feud
of the cobra sea and the mongoose wind
you must fare to reach us
through hiss and throttle come
where the great ships are scattered twigs
on a green commotion
where the plane is a fugitive mote
in the stare of the sun
Come by a limbo of motion humbled
under cliffs of cloud
and over gargantuan whalehalls
In this lymph's abyss a billion
years of spawning and dying have passed *fishing*
and will pass without ministration of man
For all the red infusions of sailors
veins of vikings lost and matelots
haemoglobin of Gilbert's hearties and Jellicoe's
for all blood seeping from corvette and sealer
from sodden hulls of *Hood* and *Titanic*
still do these waves when the gale snaps them
fracture white as the narwhal's tusk
Come then trailing whatever pattern
of gain or solace and think no more than you must
of the simple unhuman truth of this emptiness
that down deep below the lowest pulsing
of primal cell
tar-dark and dead
lie the bleak and forever capacious tombs of the sea

Grand Banks 1945

Insignificance of man to the sea?

TRANSCONTINENTAL

Crawling across this sometime garden
now in our trainbeds like clever nits
in a plush caterpillar should we take time
to glance from our dazzle of magazines
and behold this great green girl grown sick
with man   sick with the likes of us?

Toes mottled long ago by soak of seaports
ankles rashed with stubble
belly papulous with stumps?
And should we note where maggoting miners
still bore her bones to feed our crawling host
or consider the scars across her breasts
the scum of tugs upon her lakeblue eyes
the clogging logs within her blood—
in the doze between our magazines?

For certainly she is ill   her skin
is creased with our coming and going
and we trail in her face the dark breath of her dooming

She is too big and strong perhaps to die
of this disease but she grows quickly old
this lady   old with us—
nor have we any antibodies for her aid
except our own.

New Brunswick 1945

36

MAN ON A TRACTOR

What does he think
that man on a tractor
unrolling the earth's flesh
in multiple ribands behind him?
Sometimes perhaps he reckons
while rhythmic spirals of dust whirl to his throat
the hours and their fractions
till by the well he can hose his puckering skin
    By God it's going to be different now
    with a wife at the end of day
    and turning my own soil

His thoughts jog back through the burglared years
as he wheels at a corner and faces
across the coulee the barn of his old boss
remembers the long oilcloth at supper
busy with flies and chewing
the draggletailed farmwife doling old ham and custard
This is better for sure
though the brute sun
burns him still on the naked land
and the light will dim before the chores of the day are done

[handwritten margin note: Has his own farm Probably purchased with gains from the war]

Yet the throb of the iron seat
blurs in his mind with the days when he bruised his bones
driving in lines more devious
clamouring over Italian cobbles or scrub or bodies
rocking as he coughed in the fumes and waited
a shell's conclusion
Peering through olives he sometimes had fancied a flash
of chequered Albertan stubble or dreamt from a ruin
the gasoline hatbox marking the lay of this town
where the giant nostril of war inhaled and exhaled him
    Now with the prairie breeze around me
    why do I daydream of tanks
    and gulping compo with buddies
    scattered forever or dead?

[handwritten margin note: In Italy dreamed of Alberta. In Alberta memory returns to war]

He loved that clanking demon no more than the shark
is loved by its pilot-fish
What does he want?
Does he need for ever to hunt and be hunted?
    I have come through with my hands and feet
    and won the right to plow black earth of my own
yet sprouting thicker than wheat, he thinks,
are the towers of its traders

And now the shake of the tractor blurs to the flatcar
he and his brother rode through the stammering prairie
into the fountaining woods and the mountains
They had watched the olive lakes unreel
and the flying rivers milked
with the grist of the glaciers
inching down from the dazzling peaks
    Could it be only eight years ago
    that we munched a stale handout
    planned against yardbulls ahead
    and shivering envied even the trees
    that could shed their ragged clothes in the autumn
    and sleep indifferent to jobs or an empty belly?

Envying more the tourists moving among the spruce
the peacock Americans riding through resinous woods
the glistening girls in canoes on the cool lakes
For their faces were dustless and blank with ignorance
of tractors or kicks in the rump or three-day hungers
    Something the kid said as we jolted along
    "It's because of them that we're here"
    We squabbled then while the train puffed up the pass
    I called him a red "You can't blame tourists
    They're just lucky that's all; our time will come"

While the heat of the pedal soaks through his boot
this plowman eats old words in the dust
They'll be there again, he thinks, the shining faces
the chosen few who sleep in the summer mountains
eyes innocent now of tanks as then of tractors
and ears unpierced by the whistle of cop or bomb
    But the kid's luck held no farther than Caen

Farming is great but there is another world out there.

fond memories of home - away from home

Envy of tourists free from war

brother died at Caen

It's not the tourists, he knows, who've robbed him
first of a job and food and then of his brother—
but their lives are consent to all that has been
They live by the throb of this iron in his chest
by the alternation of tractor, boxcar and tank
that others ride and sweat and hunger and die in
while the sleek and their children paddle the glittering rivers
and fish by the friendly fir through a summer's glory
then wing as easy as birds to the soft south
when poplars blazon the long winter's assault

> "You just want what they have" I cracked at the kid
> And so by Christ why not?
> I'd like to see chalets for farmhands
> and the boys who are left of the tank troop
> There's room enough in the mountains
> for them and for tourists

Yet he knows as he turns at the south fence and sees
an oil truck flouring up dust on the section road

> it's not mountains I want nor buddies
> but to feel it won't happen all over again

If the crops from these smoking furrows
the ache in his back, the smile of his wife
were lines in the map of a reasoned future
without booby traps and hidden mortars of class
and the doom forever poised in the world's heaven
then could he sit resolute on this tractor as once in a tank
and the bones of his brother have meaning

And perhaps his moods as he peels the expectant earth
are not so odd to some of his troop
who bore again with agued drills in the damp of mines
or leap to couple treacherous freightcars
or twist the bolts on other tractors for other farmers

but strange no doubt these thoughts of a man on a tractor
to some of the cool tourists
moving on hired ponies under the poised avalanche

Train from Medicine Hat 1945

[handwritten margin notes:] tourist vs laborer · wants peace · If the future was secure his past would have meaning · If you weren't there it is hard to understand — you are a tourist

This is the case of a high-school land,
dead-set in adolescence;
loud treble laughs and sudden fists,
bright cheeks, the gangling presence.
This boy is wonderful at sports
and physically quite healthy;
he's taken to church on Sunday still
and keeps his prurience stealthy.
He doesn't like books, except about bears,
collects new coins and model planes,
and never refuses a dare.
His Uncle spoils him with candy, of course,
yet shouts him down when he talks at table.
You will note he's got some of his French mother's looks,
though he's not so witty and no more stable.
He's really much more like his father and yet
if you say so he'll pull a great face.
He wants to be different from everyone else
and daydreams of winning the global race.
Parents unmarried and living abroad,
relatives keen to bag the estate,
schizophrenia not excluded,
will he learn to grow up before it's too late?

Ottawa

40

THE EBB BEGINS FROM DREAM

Decline

The stars like stranded starfish pale and die
and tinted sands of dawning dry
The ebb begins from dream   leaving a border
of morning papers on the porches

From crusted reefs of homes   from unkempt shores
the workers slip reluctant   half-asleep
lapse back into the city's deep
The waves of factory hands and heads   of salesman
eyes and waiting waitress faces
slide soughing out from night's brief crannies
suck back along the strand of streets
rattling pebbled smalltalk

O then the curves and curls
of girl stenographers
the loops and purls
of children foaming in the ooze
that by the ceaseless moon of living moves
through heaving flats of habit down the day

stenographers

children

And late   from tortuous coves   remoter bays
there sets the sinuous undertow
of brokers   and the rolling politicians flow
to welter in the one pelagic motion

— stock market

Housewives   beached like crabs in staling pools
crisscross   are swashed in search of food
down to the midtown breakers' booming

women shoppers

At last with turning earth   relentless moon
slow but flooding comes the swell once more
with gurge and laughter's plash and murmur
back to the fraying rocks   far-freighted now
with briny flotsam of each morning vow

a wrack of deeds that dulls with neaping
dead thoughts that float again to sea
salt evening weeds that lie
and rot between the cracks of life
and hopes that waterlogged will never link
with land   but will be borne until they sink

Now tide is full and sighing creeps
into the clean sought coigns of sleep
And yet in sleep begins to stir
to mutter in the dark its yearning
and to the round possessive mother turning
dreams of vaster wellings
makes the last cliff totter
cradles all the globe in swaying water

The ebb begins from dream. . . .

Toronto 1945/Eaglecliff 1947

FROM THE HAZEL BOUGH *Branch*

I met a lady
    on a lazy street
hazel eyes
    and little plush feet

her legs swam by
    like lovely trout
eyes were trees
    where boys leant out

hands in the dark and
    a river side
round breasts rising
    with the finger's tide

she was plump as a finch
    and live as a salmon
gay as silk and
    proud as a Brahmin *socially cultivated older new Eng family*

we winked when we met
    and laughed when we parted
never took time
    to be brokenhearted

but no man sees
    where the trout lie now
or what leans out
    from the hazel bough

Military Hospital, Toronto 1945/Vancouver 1947

a young girl exposes her soul but as age takes over so does secrecy?

43

Not the cougar leaping to myth
from the orange lynx of our flame
not the timber swooning to death
in the shock of the saw's bright whine
but the rotograved lie
and a nursery of crosses abroad

Not the death of the prairie grass
in the blind wheat's unheeding
but the harvest mildewed in doubt
and the starved in the hour of our hoarding
not the rivers we foul but our blood
o cold and more devious rushing

Man is a snow that cracks
the trees' red resinous arches
and winters the cabined heart
till the chilled nail shrinks in the wall
and pistols the brittle air
till frost like ferns of the world that is lost
unfurls on the darkening window

Elphinstone, B.C. 1946

ULYSSES

Make no mistake sailor the suitors are here
    and the clouds not yet quiet
Peace the bitchy Queen is back
    but a captive still on shelter diet
The girl of your heart has been knitting long
    the boy-friends have arms there may be a riot
Go canny of course but don't go wrong
    there's no guarantee of an epic ending
Your old dog Time prone on the dungpile
    offers the one last whick of his tail
while you amble by not daring to notice
    and the phony lords grow fat on your ale

Soldier keep your eye on the suitors
    have a talk with your son and the old hired man
but the bow is yours and you must bend it
    or you'll never finish what Homer began

Toronto 1946

DAYBREAK ON LAKE OPAL: HIGH ROCKIES

as
the
fire
from
opals
a trem
-ulous
dawn be-
gins its
ceremony of
s l o w touch
without palms
its breath with-
out breathing along
the whorled turrets
moving shimmering fall
-ing over the scarred for
-ever-by-the-wind-besieged
ramparts the icecracked tree-
breached walls   the light of
the untouchable Sun sliding from
skyblue into the chill broken flesh
of our lifedrop   warming freeing the
silence of jays and firtops   sending a
heather of wind over unfolding asters and
eaglets   ruffling the moated lake to a green
soul and rolling once more the upraised sacrifice
of our world into the sword of Its P R E S E N C E

1946/1970

WINTER SATURDAY

Furred from the farmhouse
like caterpillars from wood
they emerge   the storm blown out
and find in the car their cocoon
Through hardening dusk and over
the cold void impelled they move
to dreams of light and sound
Over drifts like headlands they go
drawn to the town's pink cloud—
gliding unamazed through snow
by the wind marbled and fluted
With tentacle headlights now
they feel the watertank   grope
with Main Street   are blissfully caught
hatch from the car like trembling moths
circle to faces   flutter to movie
throb through the dance in a sultry swoon
But lights fail   time is false
the town was less than its glow
Again in chrysalis folded
they must go lonely
drowsy back through ghosts
the wind starts from the waiting snow

Horseshoe Bay, August 1947

*farmers go to town
on a cold winter Saturday*

PACIFIC DOOR

Through or over the deathless feud
of the cobra sea and the mongoose wind
you must fare to reach us
Through hiss and throttle come
by a limbo of motion humbled
under cliffs of cloud
and over the shark's blue home
Across the undulations of this slate
long pain and sweating courage chalked
such names as glimmer yet
Drake's crewmen scribbled here their paradise
and dying Bering lost in fog
turned north to mark us off from Asia still
Here cool Cook traced in sudden blood his final bay
and scurvied traders trailed the wakes of yesterday
until the otter rocks were bare
and all the tribal feathers plucked
Here Spaniards and Vancouver's boatmen scrawled
the problem that is ours and yours
that there is no clear Strait of Anian
to lead us easy back to Europe
that men are isled in ocean or in ice
and only joined by long endeavour to be joined
Come then on the waves of desire that well forever
and think no more than you must
of the simple unhuman truth of this emptiness
that down deep below the lowest pulsing of primal cell
tar-dark and still
lie the bleak and forever capacious tombs of the sea

Lowry's "Eridanus," Dollarton 1947

CAN. LIT.
(or *them able leave her ever*)

since we'd always sky about
when we had eagles they flew out
leaving no shadow bigger than wren's
to trouble even our broodiest hens

too busy bridging loneliness
to be alone
we hacked in railway ties
what Emily* etched in bone

we French&English never lost
our civil war
endure it still
a bloody civil bore

the wounded sirened off
no Whitman wanted
it's only by our lack of ghosts
we're haunted

Spanish Banks, Vancouver 1947/1966

*Emily Dickinson

Can. Lit. has no history.

WHAT'S SO BIG ABOUT GREEN?

Something went haywire
about a hundred centuries ago
without Us there to stop it
A tilt?   the icecap melted
saltless water
blocking the gorges
drip & rot all over again

Up from the stinking seas
the corrupt South
slid the fish
The stubborn grass
crept with mice
"Life" was at it again

Our good old lava
made a last try to stop it
boiling up a rash of volcanoes
Still those hydrocarbons
came sloshing back
infecting air/soil/
lakes—like this one

"Opal" they call it—
maybe after the original colour?
"Sulphur" 'd be better
for the springs on the nearshore
still fuming & yellowing up
from the faithful magma
—the one thing that's lasted
holding off even the algae
something pure
perfumed with primal chaos

*The birth of
the Earth.*

The first deer must have come in a tremble
to drink at that Lake
noses wrinkling at the stink
Only their taut ears to tell
if a cougar moved in the tree-limbs

Before Us that was
—a few millennia of truce
between leaf, elk & wolf
waterflies, fish & the osprey
a saw-off between berries & birds
& those First Men
the Chehaylis
inching up the outlet stream
to follow sperming salmon

They paddled their dugouts slap into magic
—wounds healed in the springs
when plugged with potash
or the chemistry of belief
So their braves ferried survivors
from tribal wars on the Big River
up to the Lake of Healing
as they called it

& the unwounded waiting round
for the holy water to work
made red oxide doodles on the cliffs
The museums have snaps
taken before We started the quarry
Get-well cards they were maybe
or just "Kilroy was here"

Nobody knows now
The Chchaylis are gone
& the salmon with them
that once blocked the canyons
in a hurry to mate & die

They all went when We came
just a couple of centuries ago
—the whites   the End Men
arrived to set things straight

arrival of whitemen

First the roving Kelts like Fraser
shedding their names
& faiths on the rivers
Then the trappers bypassing Hell's Gate
to build a fort
on the Place of Healing
In ten years they'd cut down the pines
shot off the game & the Indians
caught everything wearing fur
& moved on from the silence they made

& explorers

But rain & new bush
dissolved the fort
The Lake almost won

1858   We were back
rummaging for gold
On the way north there was time
to cut the trees again
to build & stoke a steamer
ferry mules/camels/horses
& our greatgrandfathers
They rushed up to eat the gold
& died of it

Gold miners

There was another lapse
into a sort of quiet
but nothing's quiet if there's ears
& the slimy chlorophyll's at work
It's our raging Sun
that swims in the real peace
seething away with the Others
unheard & unhearable

quiet growth

In '86 the first train
rumbled through Hell's Gate
A railway really gets
a wilderness by the throat
sends fingers in
to rub the green skin off
This one just tickled the Lake
but it scratched up a fine carcinoma   *malignant tumor*
only two hours away
our grandfathers named Vancouver

They slashed in roads
ran power lines over the balding ridges
sawed the big firs into suburbs
ground small pines into Sunday Supplements   *settlements.*
& multiplied that old mephitic stink   *- pulp mills*
into a general sulphite wind

It was our fathers dammed Opal
bit out rock & gravel pits   *- resort towns*
blasted off the stumps
& hammered up a resort town
Real progress for sure
though no one believed my generation
would be smart enough to finish it

But We were
We straddled the old pool with a highriser
the Place of Healing Chalet
complete with saunas/bars/
resident European psychiatrists
& a heliport on the roof   *tourist attractions*
Copters come in hourly now
rowing ulcerous burghers
from Northamericity
to be dunked in the pool
before colour tv & sedation

Their kids buzz the lakelength
in an hour of speed (on Speed)
drag-racing round the stumps
in the yellow waters
No worry about hitting fishermen
the last mercuric trout
washed bellyupwards long ago
& theres nothing that pullulates
but algae & whatever bugs
live on in oil & shit

No trouble either for the jets
from birds—they went
with the deer & the squirrels
down to the zoos
Some say theres a berrypatch still
at the lake's end
but then some believe in sasquatches
those apemen the Chehaylis saw
on the ridges —Who knows?
You cant see ridges anymore
now that We've got the local overcast
merged with the Continental Permacloud

The peaks are still there
How do We know?   Because the geiger boys
climb up to check the waterfalls
Man they're hotter now than those old springs
but not with sulphur!
Well   so what? the cascades peter out
before they hit the Lake
which We're draining anyway

With the new instant-blasticrete
we can reclaim the bottom
for a new rocketport
then clean off the last greenery
with napalm

So what's so big about green?
It's made to rot
like flesh.   Green   :   gangrene
Bare lava's best
and cousin to the Sun
That's where Life is   genuine Life:
fire and atoms being born
What's happened here on earth
is only science fiction
a nightmare soonest over
Somebody had to get us back
in step with all the other planets

I can't help feeling sort of proud
it's We who've done it
done it all in four generations
made organic death at last
an irreversible reaction
& finished the Original Plan
before 1984

What's more We did it without help
from even one good earthquake
or a new volcano
& without using a single bomb
—just Ourselves
and
     Our kids

Harrison Lake 1949/Aberdeen 1971/Vancouver 1973

We have received our country by pollution, etc.

Ecology

TAKKAKAW FALLS *Impact of a Waterfall.*

Jupiter   Thor   how he thunders!
High in his own cloud somewhere
smashes
explodes on her upslant ledges
arcs out foaming
falls fighting—
o roaring cold down-geyser—
falls
falls gyring   flings
rain rainbows like peacock flights
vaulting the valley
His own gale rends him
heads off spray-comets
that hurl from her taut cliff
shreds even his cataract core
juggles it
struggles—holds?
falls
ho
like Woden
Zeus   *Chief. Olympian Gods*
down
terrible the bolt of him
(writhing past firs
foamdrowned to skeletons)
the hissing iced-nebulae whirl of him
crashes
batters unstayable
batters bullthroated
life-lunging
Tak
ka
kaw
batters the brown
throbbing thighs of his mountain

Out of mist meekly the stream

Milk-young he mewls in naked-green moss
bruise-purple boulders
Slickens to slope   pours
silt-turbulent through pine   races
whole to the Yoho   coils
with Columbia   wanders
the ocean tundra   climbs
by sunladders slowly to
storm
glacier
down to the
spawning
thunder

1950

POET-TREE 2

i fear that i shall never make
a poem slippier than a snake
or oozing with as fine a juice
as runs in girls or even spruce
no i wont make not now nor later
pnomes as luverlee as pertaters
trees is made by fauns or satyrs
but only taters make pertaters
& trees is grown by sun from sod
& so are the sods who need a god
but poettrees lack any clue
they just need me   & maybe you

Savary Island, B.C. 1950/Scarborough College 1966

CLIMBERS

Above the last squeal of wheels
dead-end of the highest road
lithe climbers escape leaping
through fir where chipmunks whirl
Twilight swirls at their backs
magenta hills dissolve
in faces   they curl in crypts
where stone has shelled
and doze while spires snuff out

At dawn along cherry cliffs they stalk
glimpse the peak   on a muskmelon sky
but when glaciers wake chewing
their cud of rock over striped walls
by beryl lakes climbers must shrink
to beetles on brightness   leave birdsong
to follow the spoor of goat over
blocking ramparts by chalky waters

At noon stentorian icefalls call
and hushed they move from the barred old
snow   blindly crawl to cliff's cold
comfort   up up the horny neck of desolation
till their hands bleed at last
from the spines of the crest and they lie
at the end of thrust
weak in weak air and a daze of sight
on the pointless point of the peak

And this is the beginning of space
where there is nothing to say
and no time
except to clamber down down to the road
and the long pigs of the cars squealing

Savary Island 1950

[handwritten margin notes: "Climbers leave urban life", "– insignificance of climbers", "reach mt. top", "return"]

BUSHED

He invented a rainbow but lightning struck it
shattered it into the lake-lap of a mountain
so big his mind slowed when he looked at it

Yet he built a shack on the shore
learned to roast porcupine belly and
wore the quills on his hatband

At first he was out with the dawn
whether it yellowed bright as wood-columbine
or was only a fuzzed moth in a flannel of storm
But he found the mountain was clearly alive
sent messages whizzing down every hot morning
boomed proclamations at noon and spread out
a white guard of goat
before falling asleep on its feet at sundown

When he tried his eyes on the lake   ospreys
would fall like valkyries
choosing the cut-throat
He took then to waiting
till the night smoke rose from the boil of the sunset

But the moon carved unknown totems
out of the lakeshore
owls in the beardusky woods derided him
moosehorned cedars circled his swamps and tossed
their antlers up to the stars
then he knew   though the mountain slept   the winds
were shaping its peak to an arrowhead
poised

And now he could only
bar himself in and wait
for the great flint to come singing into his heart

Wreck Beach 1951

ELLESMERELAND I

Explorers say that harebells rise
from the cracks of Ellesmereland
and cod swim fat beneath the ice
that grinds its meagre sands
No man is settled on that coast
The harebells are alone
Nor is there talk of making man
from ice cod bell or stone

1952

[handwritten annotations: "flower", "Ellesmereland is isolated"]

ELLESMERELAND II

And now in Ellesmereland there sits
a town of twenty men
They guard the floes that reach to the Pole
a hundred leagues and ten
These warders watch the sky watch them
The stricken hills eye both
A mountie visits twice a year
and there is talk of growth

1965

[handwritten annotation: "arrival of man"]

SIX-SIDED SQUARE: ACTOPAN

Do tell me what the ordinary Mex
Madam, there is a plaza in Actopan
where ladies very usual beside most rigid hexagrams
of chili peppers squat this moment
and in Ottomíac gutturals not in Spanish lexicons
gossip while they scratch there in the open

    But arent there towns in Mexico more av—? Dear Madam,
    Actopan is a town more average than mean.
    You may approach it on a sound macadam, *pavement*
    yet prone upon the plaza's cobbles will be seen
    a brace of ancients, since no edict has forbidden,
    under separate sarapes in a common mescal dream—
    drug or liquor

    *But someone has to work to make a—*Lady,
    those ladies work at selling hexametric chili,   *women sell chili*
    and all their husbands, where the zocalo is shady,
    routinely spin in silent willynilly   *husbands make rope*
    lariats from cactus muscles; as they braid they
    hear their normal sons in crimson shorts go shrilly

bouncing an oval basketball about the square—
You mean that all the younger gener—?
I mean this is a saint's day, nothing rare,
a median saint, a medium celebration,   *having a holiday*
while pigeon-walking down the plaza stair   *in Mexican style*
on tiny heels, from hexahemeric concentration   *- forget influence of foreigners*

within the pyramidal church some architect
of Cortés built to tame her antecedents—
You mean that Mexico forgets her histor—? Madam, I suspect
that patterns more complex must have precedence:
she yearns to croon in Harlem dialect
while still her priest to Xipe prays for intercedence.

Actopans all are rounded with the ordinary
and sexed
much as they feel. *You mean—*
they are more hex-
agon and more extraordinary
than even you, dear lady, or than Egypt's queens.

1955

IRAPUATO

Mexico a conquered people

For reasons any
         brigadier
             could tell
this is a favourite
        nook
           for massacre
Toltex by Mixtex Mixtex by Aztex
Aztex by Spanishtex Spanishtex by Mexitex
by Mexitex   by Mexitex   by Texaco   by Pemex

So any farmer can see how the strawberries
are the biggest
        and reddest
            in the whole damn continent
but why
        when arranged
           under the market flies
do they look like small clotting hearts?

1955

PACHUCAN MINERS

All day in a night of lurch   blast
bend   they have deepened the dark search
their precortesian priests began
into the cold peak's argent
mysteries   Only the ore has risen
into the tasselled wind and run
on singing rails beneath the ardent
sky to sorceries beyond their vision
But now another nugget sun
himself is floated out of thought
and   Orphic and helmeted as divers
are pressed upwards all the miners

Under thin stars by murky troughs
white-eyed they spit   wash rockscurf off
turn without rancour from the guarded gate
below the white Olympus of the gringos
Helmed still and wordless they tramp down
base-metalled roadways to the town
stop where peons by their braziers
shiver to sell them roasted maize
Yet like a defeated army still
descend past blackened walls above
the tree-abandoned valley till
at the lowest street the doors of light

peal out   tequila is a brightness
in the throat   bottles and faces gleam
receive them in a sensible dream
In the cantinas helmets roll
backs fling upright   O now legs are male
are braced   each knotty pair   to hold
up song and hurl it at the night
then step their own way down to where
deep in her torchy den
snakes Toltecan looping in her ears
her crucifix agleam above the sheet
Eürydice lies and hears
the wild guitars   and daily waits
the nightly rescue of her silver men.

México 1955.

SESTINA FOR THE LADIES OF TEHUÁNTEPEC

"*Teh.* has six claims to fame: its numerous hotsprings
(*radioactive, therapeutic*); moderate earthquakes
(*none in several years*); herbivorous iguanas
(*eaten stewed*); Dictator Porfirio Diaz
(*d. 1911*); its hundred-mile-wide isthmus;
and the commanding beauty of its Indian women."

Stately still and tall as gilliflowers the women
though they no longer glide unwary past the hotsprings
naked as sunlight to each slender softer isthmus
now that ogling busloads (*Greyhound*) make their earth quake
And still skirt-bright before the flaking palace of old Diaz
(*hotel*) they gravely offer up their cold iguanas

Their furtive men (*unfamed*)   who snare iguanas
sliding on tree-limbs olive-smooth as are their women's
have fallen out of peonage to landlord Diaz
into an air more active than their tepid hotsprings
more prompt with tremors than the obsolete earthquakes
rumbling through their intercontinental isthmus

From the stone music of their past the only isthmus
from astronomic shrines fantastic as iguanas
to this unlikely world (*3 bil.*) that waits its earthquake
is their long matriarchal ritual of women
whose eyes from fires more stubborn than under hotsprings
flash out a thousand Mayan years before a Diaz

Goldnecklaced   turbaned   swaying in the square of Diaz
volute and secret as the orchids in their isthmus
braids black and luminous as obsidian by hotsprings
beneath their crowns of fruit   and crested live iguanas
rhythmic and Zapotecan-proud the classic women
dance (*v. marimbas*) their ancient therapy for earthquakes

O dance   and hurl flamboya   till the cobbled earth quakes
let your strong teeth shine out in the plaza lost to Diaz
toss your soaring sunflower plumes   sunflowering women!
Hold for all men yet your supple blossoming isthmus
lest we be noosed   consumed with all iguanas
and leave the radiant leaping of the lonely hotsprings

Beneath all hotsprings lie the triggered earthquakes
Within this gray iguana coils another Diaz
Is there a green isthmus walking yet in women?

Salina Cruz, México 1956

*The ladies have not changed
even though the society has*

SINALÓA

Si señor, is halligators here, your guidebook say it,
si, jaguar in the montañas, maybe helephants, quién sabe?
You like, dose palmas in the sunset? Certamente very nice,
it happen each night in the guía tourista
But who de hell eat jaguar, halligator, you heat em?
Mira my fren, wat dis town need is muy big breakwater—
   I like take hax to dem jeezly palmas.

So you wan buy machete? Por favor I give you
sousand machetes you give me one grand bulldozer, hey?
Wat dis country is lack, señor, is real good goosin,
is need pinehapple shove hup her bottom
(sure, sure, is bella all dose water-ayacints)
is need drains for sugarcane in dem pitoresco swamps—
   and shoot all dem anarquista egrets.

*Tourists have done little to aid the people of
Mex. They want industry to progress*

Hokay, you like bugambilla, ow you say, flower-hung cliffs?
Is ow old, de Fort? Is Colhuan, muy viejo, before Moses, no?
Is for you, señor, take em away, send us helevator for w'eat.
It like me to see all dem fine boxcar stuff full rice,
sugar, flax, rollin down to dose palmstudded ports
were Cortés and all dat crap (you heat history?)—
   and bugger de pink flamingos.

Amigo, we make you present all dem two-wheel hoxcart,
you send em Québec, were my brudder was learn to be padre—
we take ditchdiggers, tractors, Massey-Arris yes?
Sinalóa want ten sousand mile irrigation canals,
absolutamente. Is fun all dat organ-cactus fence?
Is for de birds, señor, is more better barbwire, verdad?—
   and chingar dose cute little burros.

Sin argumento, my fren, is a beautiful music,
all dem birds. Pero, wy you no like to ear combos,
refrigerator trucks? Is wonderful on straight new ighway,
jampack wit melons, peppers, bananas, tomatoes, si, si. . . .
Chirrimoyas? Mangos? You like! Is for Indios, solamente,
is bruise, no can ship, is no bueno, believe me, señor—
   and defecar on dose goddam guidebook.

Mazatlán, México 1956

MEMORY NO SERVANT

but a stubborn master

Eight years ago   weekend in Veracruz
It was sugary hot   no doubt
I'm sure my bed was a hammock
cocooned in cheesecloth

Oleander?   There must have been . . .
past the fountains down to the sea
which I rather think was too warm
. . . or were they hibiscus?
Somebody else recalls that the meals
were good   and cheap
I have some colour slides that surprise me
with improbable cascades
of bugambilla between copas de oro

But what I can be sure not to forget:
     Ten feet from the first bridge
     on the highway north from the town
     a turtle coming up from the Gulf
     Both right wheels ran over its middle
     The sound   a crushed carton
     Looking back—
     the untouched head
     ancient   stretched   and still
     moving

México 1956/Ithaca, N.Y. 1963

Has forgotten the wonderful details of his holiday but remembers the unnecessary killing of a turtle.

67

ALUROID

Blurred in a blot
of laburnum leaves
panther taut
the small Siamese
has willed even her tail's
tip to an Egyptian frieze

But not her two
sapphire burning blue
pools whose planetary bale
to the topmost wren glares through

The silent ritual she brings
they shatter   by their shrill
profanities deny
her lethal godhood
till Bast in anguish springs
her tawny grace at nothing

drops unfelicitous upon
the powermowed lawn
a staring failure
chittering

Dish clinks
and in a breath
she is a fawn
cat   house-intent
Bast's thirty teeth are masked
The terrible fires sink
to almond innocence

The wrens fly off to other deaths

Vancouver 1958

Siamese cat tries to catch a wren.
fails
returns to house to be fed.

68
— lost ability to hunt through
domestication.

TWENTY-THIRD FLIGHT

Lo as I pause in the alien vale of the airport
fearing ahead the official ambush
a voice languorous and strange as these winds of Oahu
calleth my name and I turn to be quoited in orchids
and amazed with a kiss perfumed and soft as the *lei*
Straight from a travel poster thou steppest
thy arms like mangoes for smoothness
o implausible shepherdess for this one aging sheep
and leadest me through the righteous paths of the Customs
in a mist of my own wild hopes
Yea though I walk through the valley of Immigration
I fear no evil   for thou art a vision beside me
and my name is correctly spelled
and I shall dwell in the Hawaiian Village Hotel
where thy kindred prepareth a table before me
Thou restorest my baggage   and by limousine leadest me
to where I may lie on coral sands by a stream-lined pool

Nay but thou stayest not?
Thou anointest not my naked head with oil?
O shepherdess of Flight Number Twenty-three only
thou hastenest away on thy long brown legs to enchant
thy fellow-members in Local Five of the Greeters' Union
or that favoured professor of Commerce mayhap
who leadeth thee into higher courses in Hotel Management
O nubile goddess of the Kaiser Training Programme
is it possible that tonight my cup runneth not over
and that I shall sit in the still pastures of the lobby
whilst thou leadest another old ram in garlands past me
and   bland as papaya   appearest not to remember me?
And that I shall lie by the waters of Waikiki   and want?

Honolulu 1958

Hawaiian woman meets plane — keeps tourist to hotel

Greeting over — loneliness sets in.

It's all in a days work.

WIND-CHIMES IN
A TEMPLE RUIN

This is the moment
    for two glass leaves
dangling dumb
    from the temple eaves
This is the instant
    when the sly air breathes
and the tremblers touch
    where no man sees
Who is the moving
    or moved is no matter
but the birth of the possible
    song in the rafter
that dies as the wind goes
    nudging other
broken eaves
    for waiting lovers

Nara, Japan 1958

A WALK IN KYOTO

all week   the maid tells me   bowing
her doll's body at my mat   is Boys' Day
also please Mans' Day   & gravely
bends deeper   the magnolia sprig in my alcove
is it male   the old discretions of Zen
were not shaped for my phallic western eye
there is so much discretion
in this small bowed body of an empire
(the wild hair of waterfalls combed straight
in the ricefields   the inn-maid retreating
with the face of a shut flower)   i stand hunched
& clueless   like a castaway in the shoals of my room

when i slide my parchment door to stalk awkward
through lilliput gardens framed & untouchable
as watercolours   the streets look much as everywhere
men are pulled past on the strings
of their engines   the legs of boys
are revolved by a thousand pedals
& all the faces are taut & unfestive as Moscow's
or Toronto's   or mine

Lord Buddha help us all there is vigour enough
in these islands & in all islands reefed & resounding
with cities   but the pitch is high   high as the ping
of cicadas (those small strained motors concealed
in the propped pines by the dying river) & only male
as the stretched falsetto of actors mincing the roles
of kabuki women   or female only as the lost heroes
womanized in the Ladies' Opera—
where in these alleys jammed with competing waves
of signs in two tongues & three scripts
can the simple song of a man be heard?

by the shoguns' palace   the Important Cultural Property
stripped for tiptoeing schoolgirls   i stare
at the staring penned carp that flail
on each others' backs to the shrunk pools edge
for the crumb this non-fish tossed
is this the Day's one parable
or under that peeling pagoda the 500 tons
of hermaphrodite Word?

at the inn i prepare to surrender again
my defeated shoes to the bending maid   but suddenly
the closed lotus opens to a smile & she points
to where   over my shoulder   above the sagging tiles
tall in the bare sky & huge as Gulliver
a carp is rising   golden & fighting
thrusting its paper body up from the fist
of a small boy on an empty roof   higher
& higher   into the endless winds of the world

1958

BANGKOK BOY

On the hot
cobbles hoppity
he makes a jig up
this moppet
come alive from chocolate
sudden
with all
small
boys'
joy
dancing under the sun
      that dances
      over the toy king's
      claw roofed palace
      and blazes the roof
      above the latest Hong Kong girlies
      imported to strip
      to the beat of copulation
      and shimmers the broken-china towers
      where ten thousand Buddhas
      sit forever
      on other boys' ashes
In his own time
naked
laughing he
on the scene's edge
like a small monkey-
man
in the endless Ramayana fresco
skips

that frozen fresco
of old wars
under still another glittering Wat
where tourists worship
in a regalia
of cameras
pacing out their grave
measures
along the enormous stone-still
god
or splaying
to immortalize
the splayed gyrations
of temple dancers
Beat out
brown smallfry
beat out your own
wild
jive
under this towering strayed
tourist and his bright
strange
cold—whee!—
coin in your small paws
before in his own motions
he vanishes
in the fearful tempo of a taxi
to that spireless palace
where god-tall
in their chalked goblin-faces
all tourists return
to plod in pairs like water-buffalo
by a bare hotel pool
to their funeral music

Prance
this dazzled instant
of your father's big
Buddha smile
and all the high
world bang in tune
the bright
sun caught
cool
      before in the high world's
      clumpings
      you are caught
      slid lethewards
      on choleric canals
      to where the poles of klongs
      and rows of paddyfields
      are shaped to bend
      small leaping backs
      and the flat bellies
      of impets
      are rounded with beriberi
Scamper little Thai
hot on these hot stones
scat
leap
this is forever O for
all gods' sakes
beat out
that first
last
cry of joy
under the sun!

1958

*Dance young man
before the Truth
of the real world
take away your
joy*

THE BEAR ON THE DELHI ROAD

Unreal   tall as a myth
by the road the Himalayan bear
is beating the brilliant air
with his crooked arms
About him two men   bare
spindly as locusts   leap

One pulls on a ring
in the great soft nose   His mate
flicks   flicks with a stick
up at the rolling eyes

They have not led him here
down from the fabulous hills
to this bald alien plain
and the clamorous world   to kill
but simply to teach him to dance

They are peaceful both   these spare
men of Kashmir   and the bear
alive is their living   too
If   far on the Delhi way
around him galvanic they dance
it is merely to wear   wear
from his shaggy body the tranced
wish forever to stay
only an ambling bear
four-footed in berries

It is no more joyous for them
in this hot dust to prance
out of reach of the praying claws
sharpened to paw for ants
in the shadows of deodars
It is not easy to free
myth from reality
or rear this fellow up
to lurch   lurch with them
in the tranced dancing of men

Srinagar 1958/Île des Porquerolles 1959

THE SHAPERS: VANCOUVER

1

a hundred million years
for mountains to heave
suffer valleys
the incubus of ice
grow soil-skin

twenty thousand for firs to mass
send living shafts out of the rock

2

with saw of flame
vice of thong
jade axe
the first builders contrived their truce
with sea & hill

out of high cedar slid the longboats
out of sweet wood the windsilvered homes
set tight against the rain's thin fingers
a prose for endurance

out of human fear & joy
came the Shapes beyond lust
the Fin totemic
the incomputible rhythms
the song beyond need

3

set down a century only
for the man on the spar-top
the pelt of pavement
quick thicket of boxes
the petrified phalli
out of the stone

in the screaming chainsaws
we hushed the old dreamers
in the hullabaloo of bulldozers
dynamite dynamo crane dredge combustion
buried them deeper than all compution

walking alone now
in the grandiloquent glitter
we are lost for a way
for a line
bent for the mere eye's pleasure
a form beyond need

is there a rhythm drumming from vision?
shall we tower into art   or ashes?

it is our dreams will decide
& we are their Shapers

Point Grey 1958/Kitsilano 1968

TAVERN BY THE HELLESPONT

What I want is not the flattery
of a second brandy
from the square hand
of this perfunctory Kurd
nor even Alexander's non-coms bodying
from the heavy air of history
If I could bridge their Greek
and they came chattering and dust-red from Asia
to these wharfstones
a tipsy Xenophon in tow
we would sit single
to the radio's jazz

Flailing beyond the swarthy strait
is that isolated light
they call Leander's still
but I'm no Hero
not of either sex
and do not look to see
love swimming naked toward me out of story
nor to be companioned
in a passionate terror
by resonance of bronze
or musket's blatter
beyond those yellow lamps
that peter out
below the solitary stars
to Troy

Is it for a better poet
longer swimmer
that I linger
holding like a cold sea-stone
in this smouldering Byzantium night
my loneliness?

If he should re-emerge
shake his wet arrogance off
sway on a lordly clubfoot
to my table's other chair
what would he stretch me
in the way of friendship
beyond the hand
that carved his unaccompanied name
deep in Poseidon's firmest pillar on Cape Sounion?
"Byron" was here
Duke Humphrey
Haliburton
Childe Kilroy
and are not now

Nor is that singular woman
though she casts such subtle guesses
in her throaty English
that her yoke of forlorn tourists
squeal in soft delight
and think her priestess eyes are doubly real
as television
"We caint keep no secrits from you, ma'am
Ah tail you, yore a spy!"
But what they might reveal
they do not know

Between the individual tables
couples
uncoupled by the radio's decision
turn to their true oneness
which is loneness
and pairing is how it multiplies

To remember this
is all the strength I have
for pacing other swimmers
solo in the uncrossed gulf

Istanbul 1958/Toronto 1974

FIRST TREE FOR FROST

When I was five   before the freeze went deep
my father dug me from the bush a sleeping
spruce   all greenness and limp claws
We planted it beside the gate to grow
with me   Her crown was just below my nose

But all she did that endless winter was
to make herself a cave of snow   and doze
When ground came back I topped her by my lips
In June she seemed to waken at the tips
Just keep it watered   even spruce must drink
my father said   Right through the summer's heat
I lugged jam-bucketsfull and watched my giving sink
down to those feet I could not see
That water was so cold it curled my hands
I felt the needles chilling on my tree
I stole hot kettle water   suds from pans
but those stiff branches never stirred for me
No prayers or heavings   nothing could begin
for all my care   to lift her past my chin

Then the white frosts crept back   I took
to slipping out when no one looked
and poured the steaming crescent of my pee
over the shivering body of my tree
That brown offering seemed to satisfy—
a warm tan mounted to her head

My father never understood   no more than I
why one day suddenly we found it dead
I've let trees go their own way since
Some things my loving never has convinced

Idaho State University 1960

EL GRECO: *ESPOLIO*

The carpenter is intent on the pressure of his hand

on the awl   and the trick of pinpointing his strength
through the awl to the wood   which is tough
He has no effort to spare for despoilings
or to worry if he'll be cut in on the dice
His skill is vital to the scene   and the safety of the state
Anyone can perform the indignities   It's his hard arms
and craft that hold the eyes of the convict's women
There is the problem of getting the holes exact
(in the middle of this elbowing crowd)
and deep enough to hold the spikes
after they've sunk through those bared feet
and inadequate wrists he knows are waiting behind him

He doesn't sense perhaps that one of the hands
is held in a curious gesture over him—
giving   or asking   forgiveness?—
but he'd scarcely take time to be puzzled by poses
Criminals come in all sorts
as anyone knows who makes crosses
are as mad or sane as those who decide on their killings
Our one at least has been quiet so far
though they say he talked himself into this trouble
a carpenter's son who got notions of preaching

Well here's a carpenter's son who'll have carpenter sons
God willing   and build what's wanted
temples or tables   mangers or crosses
and shape them decently
working alone in that firm and profound abstraction
which blots out the bawling of rag-snatchers
To construct with hands   knee-weight   braced thigh
keeps the back turned from death

But it's too late now for the other carpenter's boy
to return to this peace before the nails are hammered

Point Grey 1960

VILLANELLE

What shall I do with all my sea
your sun and moon have set alight
till you will swim along with me?

Its day, that lives outlandish free,
the flakes that fall within its night—
what will I do with all my sea?

How long on earth a refugee,
how far from water take the flight
till you have willed to swim with me?

Your room walls off transplendency.
These shores, the rising rocks, are bright—
what may I do with all my sea?

The strong day crumbles on the quay,
the windrows waste across the bight
till you will swim along with me.

I dive alone and grope to see
what salt and tidal things we might
but cannot reach with all our sea
till you have willed to swim with me.

Bowen Island 1961

SIXTH GRADE BIOLOGY QUIZ
(answers supplied by a rat)

To what order do the rats belong?
    To a superior order.
Where do they make their homes?
    In shelters underground
    below your lethal border.
How are their children born?
    From hydrocarbon links like yours
    but harder.
What do they eat?
    Your world's unguarded larder.
Why are they dangerous to human health?
    Because your health is our chief danger.
Have they any use for science?
        Yes, we trust in science, rodent science.
        Beneath your lab, your launching pad, your manger
        we carry on our underground research
        and learn more ways to multiply and wait
        till men have cleared themselves
        and cats
        and left the streets to glare at sky
        and there is freedom to preside
        for rats

Lieben 1961

BILLBOARDS BUILD FREEDOM OF CHOICE
—Courtesy, Oregon Chambers of Commerce—

(billboard on coastal highway)

Yegitit?
Look see
       AMERICA BUILDS BILLBOARDS
so billboards kin bill freedoma choice
between—yeah between billbores no
       WAIT
its yedoan hafta choose no more between
say like trees and billbores lessa course
wenna buncha trees is flattint out inta
       BILLB—
yeah yegotit
youkin pick between well
hey!   see!   like dat!
       ALL VINYL GET WELL DOLLS $6.98
or—watch wasdat comin up?
       PRE PAID CAT?
       PREPAID CATASTROPHE COVERAGE
yeah hell youkin have damnear anythin
       FREE 48 INCH TV IN EVERY ROOM
see!   or   watchit!
       OUR PIES TASTE LIKE MOTHERS
yeah but look bud no chickenin out
because billbores build
       AM—
yeah an AMERICA BUILDS MORE
buildbores to bill more—
sure yugotta! yugotta have
       FREEDOM TO
hey! you doan wannem godam fieldglasses!
theys probly clouds on Mount Raneer
but not on
       MOUNT RAINIER THE BEER THAT CHEERS

and not on good old yella
> SHELL

keepin de windoff yuh from allose clammy beaches
Landscapes is for the birds fella
yegotta choose between well like
between two a de same
hell like de man said Who's got time
for a third tit? *two* parties is *Okay*
that's   DEMOC   sure but yegit three
yegot COMMIES I'm tellinyeh
is like dose damfool niggers in
in Asia someweres all tryin to be nootrul
I tellyeh treesa crowd   a crowda
godamatheisticunamericananti
> BILLBORES

yeah an yewanna help Burma?   help
> *BURMA SHAVE*

yewanna keep the longhairs from starvin?
> BUY HANDMADE TOY SOLDIERS

yegotta choose fella yegotta
choose between
> AMERICA and UN—

between KEE-RISPIES and KEE-RUMPIES
between KEE-RYEST and KEE-ROOST-SHOVE
and brother if you doan pick
> RIGHT

you better
git this heap
tahelloffn
our
> FREEWAY

1961/1962

85

I

The time is the last of warmth
and the fading of brightness
*   before the final flash and the night*

I walk as the earth turns
from its burning father
here on this lowest edge of mortal city
where windows flare on faded flats
and the barren end of the ancient English
    who tippled mead in Alfred's hall
    and took tiffin in lost Lahore
drink now their fouroclock chainstore tea
sighing like old pines as the wind turns

The beat is the small   slap   slapping
of the tide sloping   slipping
its long soft fingers into the tense
joints of the trapped seawall

More ones than twos on the beaches today
strolling   or stranded as nations
woolly mermaids   dazed on beachlogs
a kept dog   sniffing   leading his woman
Seldom the lovers   seldom as reason
They will twine indoors from now to May
or ever to never   except the lovers
of what is not city   the refugees
    from the slow volcano
    the cratered rumbling   sirening vents
    the ashen air   the barren spilling
    compulsive rearing of glassy cliff
    from city
they come to the last innocent warmth
and the fading
before the unimaginable brightness

II

The theme lies in the layers
made and unmade by the nudging   lurching
spiralling down from nothing

down through the common explosion of time
through the chaos of suns
to the high seas of the spinning air
where the shelves form   and re-form down
through cirrus to clouds on cracking peaks
to the terraced woods and the shapeless town
and its dying shapers

The act is the sliding out
to the shifting rotting
folds of the sands that lip
slipping to reefs and sinking cliffs
that ladder down to the ocean's abyss
and farther down through a thousand seas
of the mantling rock
to the dense unbeating black unapproachable
heart of this world

Lanknosed lady sits on a seawall
not alone   she sits with an older book
Who is it?   Shakespeare   Sophocles   Simenon?
They are tranced as sinners unafraid
in the common gaze to pursue
under hard covers their private
affair   though today there is no unbusy body
but me to throw them a public look

not this wrinkled triad of tourists
strayed off the trail from the rank zoo
peering away from irrelevant sea
seeking a starred sign for the bus-stop
They dangle plastic totems   a kewpie
a Hong Kong puzzle for somebody's child
who waits to be worshipped
back on the prairie farm

No nor the two manlings
all muscles and snorkels and need to shout
with Canadian voices   Nipponese bodies
racing each other into the chilling waters
last maybe of whatever summer's swimmers

Nor for certain the gamey gaffer
asleep on the bench like a local Buddha
above them   buttonedup mackinaw
Sally Ann trousers   writing in stillness
his own last book   under the squashed
cock of his hat   with a bawdy plot
she never will follow

A tremor only of all his dream
runs like fear from under the hat
through the burned face to twitch
one broken boot   at the other end
of the bench as I pass

dreaming my own unraveled plots
between eating water and eaten shore
     in this hour of the tired and homing
     retired   dissolving
     in the days of the separate wait
     for the mass dying

and I having clambered down to the last
shelf of the gasping world of lungs
do not know why I too wait and stare
before descending the final step
into the clouds of the sea

III

The beat beating is the soft cheek
nudging of the sly shoving almost
immortal ocean at work
on the earth's liquidation

Outward the sun explodes light
like a mild rehearsal of light to come
over the vitreous waters
At this edge of the blast
a young girl sits on a granite bench
so still as if already only
silhouette burned in the stone

Two women pass in a cloud of words
. . . so I said You're *not*!?
and she said I *am*!
I'm one of the Lockeys!
Not the Lockeys of *Out*garden surely
I said *Yes* she said but I live
in Winnipeg now Why for heaven's *sake*
I said then you *must* know Carl *Thors*on?
Carl? she said he's my cousin by marriage
He *is* I said why he's *mine* too! So. . . .

Born from the glare come the freakish forms
of tugs all bows and swollen funnels
straining to harbour in False Creek
and blindly followed by mute scows
    with islets of gravel to thicken the city
    and square bowls of saffron sawdust
    the ground meal of the manstruck forest
or towing shining grids of the trees stricken

At the edge of knowledge the *Prince Apollo*
   (or is it the *Princess Helen?*)
floats in a paperblue fusion of air
gulf   Mykenean islands
and crawls with its freight of flesh
toward the glare and the night waiting
behind the hidden Gate of the Lions

IV

The beat is the slap slip   nudging
as the ledges are made   unmade
by the lurching swaying of all the world
that lies under the spinning air

from the dead centre and the fiery circles
up through the ooze to black liquidities
up to the vast moats
where the doomed whales are swimming
by the weedy walls of sunless Carcassonnes
rising   rising   to the great eels waiting
in salt embrasures   and swirling up
to the twilit roofs that floor the Gulf
up to the crab-scratched sands
of the dappled Banks

into the sunblazed living mud
and the radiant mussels
that armour the rocks

   and I on the path at the high-tide edge
   wandering under the leafless maples
   between the lost salt home
   and the asphalt ledge where carhorns call
   call in the clotting air by a shore
   where shamans never again will sound
   with moon-snail conch the ritual plea
   to brother salmon or vanished seal
   and none ever heard
   the horn of Triton or merman

V

The beat is the bob   dip   dipping
in the small waves   of the ducks shoring
and the shored rocks that seem to move
from turning earth or breathing ocean
in the dazzling slant of the cooling sun

Through piled backyards of the sculptor sea
I climb   over discarded hemlock saurians
    Medusae cedar-stumps   muscled horsemen
    Tartars or Crees   sandsunk forever
and past the raw sawed butt
    telltale with brands
of a buccaneered boom-log
    whisked away to a no-question mill

all the swashing topmost reach of the sea
    that is also the deepest
    reach of wrens   the vanishing squirrel
    and the spilling city
the stinking ledge disputed by barnacles
waiting for tiderise to kick in their food
contested by jittery sandfleas
and hovering gulls that are half-sounds only
traced overhead   lone as my half-thoughts
    wheeling too with persistence of hunger
    or floating on scraps of flotsam

VI

Slowly   scarcely sensed   the beat
has been quickening now as the air
from the whitened peaks is falling
faraway sliding   pouring down
through the higher canyons and over
knolls and roofs to a oneway urgent
procession of rhythms

blowing the haze from False Creek's girders
where now I walk as the waves stream
from my feet to the bay to the far shore
where they lap like dreams that never reach

The tree-barbed tip of Point Grey's lance
has failed again to impale the gone sun
Clouds and islands float together
out from the darkening bandsaw of suburbs
and burn like sodium over the sunset waters

Something   is it only the wind?
above a jungle of harbour masts
is playing paperchase with the persons
of starlings   They sift and fall
stall and soar   turning
      as I too turn   with the need to feel
      once more the yielding of moist sand
      and thread the rocks back to the seawall

shadowed and empty now
of booklost ladies or flickering wrens
and beyond to the Boats for Hire
where a thin old Swede clings in his chair
like hope to the last light

eyeing bluely the girls with rackets
padding back from belated tennis
while herring gulls make civic statues
of three posts on the pier
and all his child-bright boats
heave unwanted to winter sleep

      Further the shore dips   and the sea   sullen
      with sludge from floors of barges   spits
      arrogantly over the Harbour Board's wall
      and only the brutish prow of something
      a troller perhaps   lies longdrowned
      on an Ararat of broken clamshells
      and the flakings of dead crabs

The shore snouts up again
spilling beachlogs glossy and dry
as sloughed snakeskins
but with sodden immovable hearts
heigh ho the logs that no one wants
and the men that sit on the logs
that no one wants
while the sea repeats what it said
to the first unthinking frogs
and the green wounds of the granite stones

By cold depths and by cliffs
whose shine will pass any moment now
the shore puts an end to my ledge
and I climb past the dried shell
of the children's pool   waiting like faith
for summer   to where the last leaves
of the shore's alders   glistening with salt
have turned the ragged lawns
to a battlefield bright with their bodies

VII

For the time is after the scarring of maples
torn by the fall's first fury of air
on the nearest shelf above brine and sand
where the world of the dry troubling begins

the first days of the vitreous fusing
of deserts   the proud irradiations of air
the clotting oceans
in the years when men rise
and fall   from the moon's ledge

while the moon sends   as before
the waters swirling up and back
from the bay's world
to this darkening bitten shore

I turn to the terraced road
the cold steps to the bland new block
the human-encrusted reefs
that rise here higher than firs or singing
up to aseptic penthouse hillforts
to antennae above the crosses
pylons marching over the peaks
of mountains without Olympus

Higher than clouds and strata of jetstreams
the air-roads wait the two-way traffic
And beyond?   The desert planets
What else?   a galaxy-full perhaps
of suns and penthouses waiting

But still on the highest shelf of ever
washed by the curve of timeless returnings
lies the unreached unreachable nothing
whose winds wash down to the human shores
and slip   shoving

into each thought nudging my footsteps now
as I turn to my brief night's ledge

in the last of warmth
and the fading of brightness
on the sliding edge of the beating sea

Vancouver 1961/Ametlla, Spain 1963

It was the hand that caught in me

Sudden as a beast the blizzard
had whirled on us   was gone
as quick over the hill and howling
through the next village   whose spire
could be glimpsed blotting out now
in a gray fury

And we are wading   a straggle of passengers
in town shoes   through a snowscape
clean and cosy as any Christmas card
the small firs like spunwhite candy
spaced on the ice-cream hillocks

Already the sunlight smoulders down
burning on the narrow tracks at the crossing
and fires the sleet that sheathes one flank
and the bland diesel-face of our train
so small and innocent now it has stopped

You wouldn't think from that little jolt we got!
. . . Speedin . . . Naw, in that storm he jes couldn see

Green as a great bruise
where the smooth flesh of the drifts
has been savaged   the auto lies
crumpled and akimbo
like a beetle battered by catspaw

Flung it fifty feet . . . Yeah an him further . . .
This year's chevvy . . . Well we stopped fast enough

Car-train crash

95

We stand   the unsilent   stamping
staring   to reduce to livable size
what is casually spreadeagled here in the snow

Should be a law about level cross—
Sure but we oughta wistled wen—Hell we did!
. . . Anybody know who he is?

We too anonymous   one to the other
but our breaths write on the air
the kinship of being alive
surrounding the perfect stranger

Christ it's too cold I'm gittin back . . .
Yep ain't nothin we kin do . . . Hey look
He's only gone three hunderd . . .

A thin man unprompted is gathering papers
slewed from a briefcase over the raddled banks
He slaps them free of flakes
and packs them carefully back in the case
Now he teeters   not knowing what to do with it
The brakeman plods up with a plaid blanket

Train gonna be held up till police come?
. . . No I'm stayin
Conductor was up to that farm phonin em

The man with the case silently lays it
next to the open palm
the blanket has failed to cover
He offers his only remark

Assizes is on up to Wolfville
Them's law papers

The halfburied engine continues to tick
with cooling   something live under the snow
Each time we are startled

engenders

no one knows who was killed

Lawyer eh? . . . Musta stalled on the track
grabbed his case got half out his door . . .
Yep nearly made it . . . Young feller too

    The sun has given way again to a black sky
    Most have tramped back to the train
    The rest of us circle about
    as if for somewhere to put down the guilt

Yer all lucky we dint go offa the tracks
. . . He's right   Can't blame the crew none

    Diesel shrieks and we jump
    The brakeman gestures   Turning at once
    we leave him beating his arms for warmth
    turn in a pleasure of hurry   to hop
    like schoolboys back in the steps we made
    eager for heat and motion   arrivals
    and shaping already what happened

    The train moves to its goal
    and scatters us from the scene forever
    The manner of hills   words   faces
    slides from the gloss protecting each mind
    We will forget even that scotched face perhaps
    waiting till the gay rug came down
    in a Christmas world

    But not surely the longfingered hand
    stretched in some arresting habit of eloquence
    to the last irrational judgement
    roaring in from the storm

    Or is it only in me that the hand hooked
    and I who must manage it now like a third?

Nova Scotia 1962

FOR GEORGE LAMMING   *White bay in black crowd. ?*

To you
    I can risk words about this

Mastering them   you know
      they are dull
         servants
who say less
    and worse
        than we feel

That party above Kingston Town
    we stood   five (six?) couples

linked singing
    more than rum happy

I was giddy
    from sudden friendship
wanted   undeserved

    black tulip faces

self swaying forgotten

    laughter in dance

Suddenly on a wall mirror
    my face assaulted me
stunned to see itself
    like a white snail
       in the supple dark flowers

Always now I move grateful
    to all of you
who let me walk thoughtless
    and unchallenged
in the gardens
    in the castles
        of your skins *

Off Haiti 1962

In the Castle of My Skin is the title of George Lamming's autobiography of his childhood as an impoverished black boy in British-colonial Barbados.

CURAÇAO

I think I am going to love it here

I ask the man in the telegraph office
the way to the bank
He locks up and walks along with me
insisting he needs the exercise

When I ask the lady at my hotel desk
what bus to take to the beach
she gets me a lift with her beautiful sister
who is just driving by in a sports job

And already I have thought of something
I want to ask the sister

1962

"Nice jacket you got dere, man"

He swerved his bicycle toward my curb
to call   then flashed round the corner
a blur in the dusk   of somebody big
redshirted   young   dark   unsmiling

As I stood hoping for a taxi to show
I thought him droll at least
A passing pleasantry?   It was frayed
a sixdollar coat   tropical weight
in this heat only something with pockets
to carry things in

Now all four streets were empty
Dockland   everything shut

It was a sound no bigger than a breath
that made me wheel

He was ten feet away   redshirt
The cycle leant by a post farther off
where an alley came in   What?!

My turning froze him
in the middle of some elaborate stealth
He looked almost comic   splayed
but there was a glitter
under the downheld hand
and something smoked from his eyes

By God if I was going to be stabbed
for my wallet (adrenalin suffused me)
it would have to be done in plain sight
I made a flying leap
to the middle of the crossing
White man   tourist   surrogate   yes
but not guilty enough
to be skewered in the guts for it
without raising all Trinidad first
with shouts   fists   feet   whatever
—I squared round to meet him

and there was a beautiful taxi
lumbering in from a sidestreet
empty!

As I rolled away   safe as Elijah
lucky as Ganymede
there on the curb I'd leaped from
stood that damned cyclist solemnly
shouting

"What did he say?"   I asked the driver
He shrugged at the windshield
"Man dat a crazy boogoo
He soun like he say
'dat a nice jump you got too' "

Port-of-Spain 1962

LETTER TO A CUZCO PRIEST

Father   whose name
your smalltown paper took in vain

Young father   whose face
blurred in the cheap newsprint
I could not recognize in a street

Father   who will never know me
nor read this   which is written
in your honour
in the terms of my worship

Father   forgive yourself

    This morning two Quechuanos
    tramped on their horny feet
    down sun-ravaged slopes
    clutching cardboard banners
    Thirty more Indians followed
    sunfaced   silent   ragged
    and as many boneknobbly goats
    maybe a hundred sheep
    gut-swollen   yammering
    Their dust rose   was carried
    by thin winds like incense
    over sculptured rocks
    that once bore up the Moon's Temple

    Dry wail of the beasts
    dropping over denuded terraces
    enchanted the ears of travellers
    lining up two Cuzco kids
    (dressed like Inca princelings
    by the Oficina de Tourismo)
    to be shot by cameras
    in front of the Bath of the Priestess

Father   worship yourself

    Where stony slopes level
    to unfenced valleys   the sheep
    took over the lead   sniffing grass
    not the boundary stakes

Father you were not with those shepherds
but your Word sent them

    A local watchman for the Lima agent
    for the American banker
    for the Peruvian landowner
    living in Madrid
    phoned the Cuzco cops
    who phoned the army regiment
    quartered locally to handle such jobs

Father   the guilt is not yours
though words that blazed last week
from your pulpit lettered their placards

    The two who bore them are dead

Father   the guilt begins
in the other pulpits and all the places
where no one will say your words

    "The Government is only
    an armed front for Fifty Families"

where no one calls on whatever his country

    "Let the land feed its people"

Father   the guilt is not that you spoke
nor that the poor listened   acted
have come again to defeat

    Twenty of those who followed
    into convenient range of the troops
    tend their own wounds
    in the jail's bullpen

Father   forgive all men if you must
but only in despite of god
and in Man's name

    Their flocks   driven back
    to the spiny heights
    are herded now by the boys and women

Do not forgive your god
who cannot change   being perfect

    Blood dries on the uncropped grass
    The goats eat dust

Father   honour your Man,
though he will not honour you
in whatever priestly purgatory
authority muffles you now

    In Cuzco the paper that quoted the sermon
    and printed your face
    today demands death
    for the Red (Indian?) spies in the Andes

Father   gullible and noble
born to be martyred
and to be the worthy instrument
of the martyrdom of the gullible

      I who am not deceived
      by your cold deity

      believe

      for there is no other belief

      in the wild unquenchable God
      flaming within you

Pray to yourself above all for men like me
that we do not quench
the Man
in each of us

Peru 1962

Flowers live here as easily as air
They hang from power lines   they grow on light
A scalloped leaflet lying on a stair
will puff pink buds   and root itself in stone—
The animal hunts by day or pads within the night

The waxy jasmine   Indian arum   red mimosa
tangle unbruised   thigh to alien thigh
the dark Ashanti Blood   the yellow roses
keep peace beneath a prism sun—
White men alone the rainbow world deny

Stubborn as coral the crimson flowers rise
The torch plant towers higher than a man
Each dawn hibiscus gaze with newmade eyes
and cereus nightly stars the jungle roof—
The other kingdom rules what roosts it can

Petal and bract outdo the stir of sky
Their silent cockatoos in every park
preen and are fed without the need to fly
Coldly they nourish birds of heat   and shelter
all bony forms that cry before the dark

Still souls of butterflies the orchids poise
about the flaming trees and are not singed
Lilies turn spiders into spirit   dragons to toys
The Passion Flower lifts its crucifix unmanned—
Only the worlds of blood on suffering are hinged

When all the life of sound has milled
to silence I think these vines will find
a way to trumpet green and purple still
and jacarandas ring their bells down ruined streets—
Our kingdom comes and goes with mind

Mona, Jamaica 1962

TRANSISTOR

She clung to the broom
a long witchy affair she'd been using
to swipe the ancient floor
of the one habitable room
when we came in for a breather
out of the jeep and the humid morning
to this guesthouse
where no one stayed any more
Eyes too bright to be plumbed
gleamed above the homemade handle
She was just tall enough to see over
and her arms   from the grip of the hands
were torsioned as burnt tree-roots
        twisted

"Like she was hol'in a mike"
the engineer's little black steno said
and giggled   drifting then to the porch
where her boy friend already had vanished
They had come along for the ride

But the old woman was belting songs out
as if she had to send them all the way
back to the sea and the canebrakes
her greatgrandfather ran from
the night he brought her words
stored in his rebellious head
beyond the howl of the slavers' hounds
to this remotest hilltop in Jamaica

In truth she'd never faced mike nor tape
Today was the first she'd seen a transistor
and she'd stared at that more with fear
than interest when the little steno
had sauntered by from the jeep with it

An anchor to keep the rest of her tiny self
from floating up level with the notes
was more what she needed the broom for
I thought   utterly stilled in my chair
under the clean power
coiled in four generations of skulls
and springing out now
from the mouth of this bird-still body

It was the engineer she sang for
because he had asked her
he always did
Yet mine was a new face
with the colour to make anyone wary
up in these mountains
So she stood poised for reversal
back to the caretaker's role

But she soon forgot me   him too
as her mind unravelled to airs
a grandmother might have woven
stooping in dappled coffee groves
when this was a plantation house
buzzing with whiteman's prospering

She paused only once   to down a glass
the engineer poured from the rum he'd brought
He knew what songs to ask for
and out they came now whorling
as if her voice were immortal and separate
within her   and she only the toughened reed
vibrated still by the singing dead
by the slaved and the half-free
The narrow high-ceilinged room was a box
resounding with all the mourning of loves
and deaths   the fear of Mamba   hope of Jesus
the bitter years and the bawdy
till suddenly   at her first falter
she seemed to listen
and stopped

It was not quite all
though my thanks alone might have sent her off
if the engineer hadn't silently offered
a second rum   The besom again in one hand
like a rifle at ease
she swung to me
and in the grave high rhythms of the Victorians
toasted my health
and that of all the gentlemen of my nation
with all the dignity of hers
then disappeared into her kitchen
broom already waggling

It was only then I let my ear tell me
there'd been a counter-bass going on all along
Out on the dusty porch I found the young pair
sitting on the rail at the farthest corner
Two faces black and anxious
leant together under the transistor
They'd found a nail in a pillar to hang it by
The morning disc spin from Puerto Rico
was sending a Hollywood cowboy
from last year's Parade
The machine swung his voice from shriek
to silence and back
I suppose they'd been listening to him
as exclusively as I to her
and out of just as much need
to exchange our pasts

Yallahs Mountain 1962

- A negress cleaning lady sings
- Author and engineer listen
- Both remin... about past
- Youth listen to cowboy.

Diff Strokes for different folks!

TORONTO BOARD OF TRADE GOES ABROAD
(Union Club, Santiago de Chile, October 1962)

George! I dunno how you *do* it George. . .

Wy, eat all at *stuff,* all at horses *doovers* after all we had for *lunch*! I bet you dunno wat half it *is*! *Raw fish* fer gossake I betitis you wanna *watch* that stuff George. Fellah in *Mexico* told me theres *worms* in it. . .

Gossake George I wish I had your *appetite* I cant *eat* I cant eat *any*thin. . .

Naw *I'm* not worryin . . . *Crisis*?!   Hell George I *never* got the wind up and you know *wy* George? Because I allus *knew* that sonfabitch *Kroo*shef had no *guts*. . .

Naw George its I gotta terrible *thirst.* Its them uh Pis—? Them. . .

Yeah *Pisscoes*! *Thats* wot they give us at lunch, yeah *hell* I thought they was kinda mild mar*teen*ies but theyre straight *al*cohol George—an an redis*tilled*! *Wow!*. . .

Four a them. . .

Yeah, so wat wouldn I give *now* for, for you know *wat* George? For jus, jus a liddle drink of *wat*er because you know somethin George? George? This the *longest bar* ina *world*. . .

Well I bet in Southa Merica anyway. . .

You take a *look,* hunderd twenny five *mee*tres fellah over there told me, blongsta Club, wy thas —how much *is* that George?

Yeah well thasa lot eh? an George every *yard* of its *piled* with *licker* analla this greazer *chow* yer eatin and you jes try find a drinka *water* on it! . . .

O sure sure but how you gonna trustim? They doenoe *ing*lish George these waiters. Anyway watta *they* care if its con*tam*inated maybe *loaded* with you know *wat* George, wat *you* got in Per*oo* George!

Well now doan get me *wrong* I wouldn let *them* hear me I'm not criticizin hell *no* these things doan really *matter* itsa great *country* and we all got somethin in *common* Canadians Chileans because you know *wot?* you know wattis we got in common? we're all A*me*ricans thas wat eh George? thas watta tellem but jussa same George I'd— George I'd give ten *bucks* this *min*ute for *one glass* of good old *Lake Ontario tapwater* thas wat—George?. . . George?!

Now where the hell did *he* git to?

CARTAGENA DE INDIAS, 1962
Ciudad triste, ayer reina de la mar (Heredia)

Each face its own phantom
its own formula of breed and shade
but all the eyes accuse me back and say

    There are only two races here:
    we human citizens
    who are poor but have things to sell
    and you   from outer space
    unseasonable   our one tourist
    but plainly able to buy

This arthritic street
where Drake's men and Cole's ran
swung cutlasses   where wine and sweet blood
snaked in the cobble's joints
    leaps now in a sennet of taxi horns
    to betray my invasion
All watch my first retreat
to barbizans patched from Morgan's grapeshot
and they rush me
    three desperate tarantula youths
waving Old Golds unexcised

By an altar blackened
where the Indian silver was scratched away
in sanctuary leaning   on lush cool marble
    I am hemmed by a conga drum-man in jeans
    He bares a brace of Swiss watches
    whispers in husky Texan

Where gems and indigo were sorted
   in shouting arcades
   I am deftly shortchanged
and slink to the trees that lean
and flower tall in the Plaza
   nine shoeboys wham their boxes
   slap at my newshined feet

Only in the Indio market
mazed on the sodden quais
I am granted uneasy truce
Around the ritual braidings of hair
the magical arrangements of fish
the piled rainbows of rotting fruit
I cast a shadow of silence
   blue-dreaded eyes
   corpse face *— member of lower nobility of Spain*
   hidalgo clothes
   tall one   tall as a demon
   pass O pass us quickly

Behind me the bright blaze of patois *— jargon — illiterate or provincial speech*
   leaps again

I step to the beautiful slave-built bridge
and a mestiza girl   *mixed Blood. European & Am. In.*
   levels Christ's hands at me
   under a dangling goiter

Past the glazed-eyed screamers of *dulces*
swing to a pink lane
where a poxed and slit-eyed savage
   pouts an obscenity
   offering a sister
   as he would spit me
   a dart from a blowpipe

Somewhere there must be another bridge
from my stupid wish
to their human acceptance
but what can I offer—
my tongue half-locked in the cell
of its language—other than pesos
    to these old crones of thirty
    whose young sink in pellagra   *desware*
    as I clump unmaimed
    in the bright shoes
    that keep me from hookworm
    lockjaw and snakebite

It's written in the cut of my glasses
I've a hotelroom all to myself
with a fan   and a box of Vitamin C
It can be measured
in my unnatural stride
that my life expectation
is more than forty
especially now that I'm close to sixty

older than ever bankrupt Bolívar was
who sits now in a frozen prance
high over the coconut trays
quivering on the heads
    of three gaunt mulatto ladies
    circling in a pavane of commerce
    down upon spotlit me

Out of the heaving womb of independence
Bolívar rode   and over the bloody afterbirth
into coffee and standard oil
    from inquisitional baroque
    to armed forces corbusier

    He alone has nothing more
    to sell me

I come routed now   scuffling
through dust in a nameless square
treeless burning deserted
come lost and guiltily wakeful
in the hour of siesta
    at last to a message

    to a pair of shoes
    in a circle of baked mud
    worn   out of shape   one on its side
For a second I am shaken by panic
heat? humidity? something has got me
    the shoes are concrete
    and ten feet long

    the sight of a plaque calms
    without telling me much

En homenaje de la memoria de
    LUIS LOPEZ
*se erigió este monumento
    a los zapatos viejos
el día 10 de febrero de 1957*

Luis Lopez? Monument to his old shoes?
What??? There was nothing else
and the square was asleep

Back through the huckster streets
the sad taxi men still begging with horns
to the one bookstore

Si señor   Luis Lopez el poeta
Here is his book
Unamuno praised it   *si si*
You have seen *los zapatos?*   Ah?
But they are us, *señor*
It was about us he wrote
about Cartagena where he was born
and died   See here this sonnet
always he said hard things about us
Said we were lazy except to make noise
and we only shout to get money
ugly too, backward . . . why not?
it is for a poet to say these things
Also he said *plena*—how say it?—
plena de rancio desaliño
Full of rancid disarray!
    Si, Si, but look at the end, when old
he come to say one nice thing
only one ever about us
He say we inspire that love a man has
for his old shoes—*entonces*
we give him a monument to the shoes

I bought the book   walked back
sat on the curb happier than Wordsworth
gazing away at his daffodils

Discarded queen   I thought   I love you too
Full of rancid disarray
city like any city
full of the stench of human indignity
and disarray of the human proportion
full of the noisy always poor
and the precocious dying
stinking with fear   the stale of ignorance
I love you first for giving birth
to Luis Lopez   suffering him
honouring him at last
in the grand laconic manner
he taught you

terseness of speech . sparing of words

—and him I envy
I who am seldom read by my townsmen

Descendants of pirates   grandees
galleyslaves and cannibals
I love the whole starved cheating
poetry-reading lot of you   most of all
for throwing me the shoes of deadman Luis
to walk me back into your brotherhood

Colombia 1962/Greece 1963

PLAZA DE LA INQUISICIÓN
(for pat)

A spider's body
limp and hairy
appeared at the bottom of my coffee

The waiter being Castilian
said passionately nothing
And why indeed should apologies
be made to me

It was I who was looking in
at the spider
It might be years
before I slipped and drowned
in somebody else's cup

Madrid 1963

EPIDAURUS

Taking the baths for their nerves
anxious Corinthian ladies
no doubt complained to the attendants
about the noise
              pedlars
                              MUSSELLLS!
                              FIGgggs!
                    donkeys
                    foot pilgrims
                    weekend chariots
all that shoving and braying
past Aesculapius' own temple
into the great new eyesore of a showplace
and the brawling out again
with torches into the night

Now everything's been put right
                    "the visitor is offered
                    every convenience   easy access
                    unlimited parking   refreshments
                    at the Tourist Pavilion
                    also a quick & comfortable
                    getaway"
and the season lasts only six weeks

After twenty-five centuries
something is also being done
about the wildflowers
flagrantly widening the cracks
in even the best seats

Everybody however
still waits to
hear the
pin
dr
o

p

Greece 1963

LOOKING FROM OREGON

"And what it watches is not our wars"
                                        (Robinson Jeffers)

Far out as I can see
into the crazy dance of light
there are cormorants like little black eyebrows
wriggling and drooping
            but the eye is out of all proportion

Nearer   just beyond the roiling surf
salmon   the young or the sperm-heavy
are being overtaken by bird's neb
sealion's teeth   fisherman's talon

The spent waters
            flecks in this corner of the eyeball
falling past my friend and his two sons
            where they straddle the groin's head
collapse on the beach
            after the long race
from where?   perhaps from Tonkin's gulf
            on the bloodshot edge

There's no good my searching the horizon
            I'm one of those another poet* saw
            sitting beside our other ocean
I can't look farther out or in

Yet up here in the wild parsnips and the wind
I know the earth is not holding
tumbles in body-lengths
towards thunderheads and unimaginable Asia

though below me on the frothy rocks
my friend and his two boys
do not look up from fishing

Florence, Oregon August 1964

*v. Robert Frost's "Neither out far nor in deep."

120

OIL REFINERY

Under the fume   of the first dragons
those spellbinders who guard   goldhoards under barrows
whole fields of warriors   wilted: even Beowulf
fell in balebreath   from firedrake fangs

Yet this hugest of Worms   though he outburst heaving
from deepest of meres   under farthest moor
is led leaping and leaping   at last to these shores
and hour by hour   overhewn and whelmed

Not without fury resists   flames in the night
blasts the world air   wans all blue day
Ho! a handful of thanes   in helmets threaten him
in silver keeps stab him   the old swartshiner
with gauges bedevil   with dials with cyclonesnuffers
endless they slaughter   that slimiest of Nadders

Hwaet! he is quick again   thousand-toothed Queller
whirls his ghost in our wheels   unleashes or locks them
Yea he twins twentyfold   twines in our graveloot
breath of that sly snake   stifles and clings
slides from our long ships   coils round our steadings
Eala! we are lost   in the spell of his loopings.

Port Moody, B.C. 1964

11 pm & sunset still going on
but that could be the latitude
whats wrongs the colour
everywhere horseshit ochre & roiling
like paper that twists/browns
before firing up on hot ashes
theres somebodys hell ahead
meantime our lips prick
& the trees are dead

but its another 20 miles before the sign
    You Are Entering
     SUDBURY
    Home of the world's largest
& christ there on the skull of a hill
3 manhattan-high stacks a phallic calvary
ejaculating some essence of rotten semen
straight up like mass sabotage at cape kennedy

the damned are all over the young
shrieking (looking much like anyone)
drag-race with radios up
from one smouldering stoplight to another—
under neon the older faces
assembled from half europe
screwcheeked/pitted all the same way
have something dignified about their devilship
that stares us down till they come human
& houck brown on the cement

   WELCOME TO . . . 73% OF THE FREE
   WORLD'S NICKEL IS CREATED HERE
& the free world invented a special cough
not even 100 taverns can dampen
nor all the jukes drown in the doorways
of pandemonium milton thou shouldst
be living etc

DEAD END   wheres west?   sunset folded
our headlights finger dumped cans
wriggle through streets like crevasses
blasted in bedrock pink & folded
like glazed guts on a butchers marble

out of the starless dark falls the roar
of golgotha   how long before one stops
noticing?   & the sting in the eyes?

by a raped old car an indian sits
praying?   puking
              You Are Leaving
                SUDBURY
         Center of Free Enterprise
& 20 more miles of battlefield

at last a moon looms up
we are into the dumb firs again
         TURN OUT   300 YDS
              HISTORIC SITE
              FRENCH RIVER
what?   canoe route the Hurons found
& showed the whites—
the way to the west   silks   buffalo
vietnam   the moon
shines over the middle of nowhere—
dumb as the trees

we stop for a leak   silence
too late for other cars
the trees listen back
nothing   the owls dead too?

suddenly some kind of low growl
coming up!   we head for the car—
only a night jet

but after it passes we realize
we'd been hearing the river all along

Northern Ontario 1965

123

THERE ARE DELICACIES
(for alison)

there are delicacies in you
    like the hearts of watches
there are wheels that turn
    on the tips of rubies
& tiny intricate locks

i need your help
    to contrive keys
there is so little time
    even for the finest
      watches

Scarborough 1965

I THINK YOU ARE A WHOLE CITY

& yesterday when i first touched
you i started moving
thru one of your suburbs
where all the gardens are fresh
with faces of you
flowering up

some girls are only houses
maybe a strip
development
woman you are miles
of boulevards with supple trees
unpruned & full of winding
honesties

so give me time   i want
i want to know
all your squares & cloverleafs
im steering now by a constellation
winking over this nights rim
from some great beachside of you
with highrisers & a spotlit
beaux arts

i can hear your beat-
ing centre   will i
will i make it
are there maps of you
i keep circling   imagining
parks fountains   your stores

back in my single bed i wander
your stranger   dreaming
i am your citizen

Waterloo 1965

Avenue Road, Toronto 1965

THE MAMMOTH CORRIDORS

From Vancouver, Canada's Pacific metropolis, the
tourist may drive east over the smooth Trans-Canada
Hiway through a

Turning from the great islands drowning
in the morning's waves from Asia
my car heads me through the city's April
    cherry petals on the slick streets
    against the flayed mountains the billboards
    conjuring perfection   Tahiti
    orgasms of power   death insurance

        thousand miles of towering Rockies to the prairies.
        Crossing from the north shore at the spectacular
        Lion's Gate, the motorist begins to trace in reverse

Over the taut bridge   through the lonely park
my wheels will themselves to the shrieking

        the spectacular route taken by the first explorers
        and hardy traders. Stanley Park, with its convenient
        thruway, aquarium, totem poles (exact replicas of
        originals now stored for preservation) . . . a thousand
        acres of playground where Indians once camped . . .

Around the highrisers   the sullen leisured
dogs   and the rolling realtors
Then the spastic traffic
of buyers and bought   pedlars of weed and soap
of acid and snow   of work and wonder
'as the world asketh'   in Skidroad's lanes

Eastward an hour and the master I own
has rushed me to winter and wildness
and merely the gray road coiling and diminishing
upward like a dragon's tail swinges me off
from the unsupportable Real
    the tortured peaks
    only a breath more broken
    the blind dive of the canyons
    a scratch of a century deeper
    since those first compulsive whites
    the Searchers
    for gold   absolution   furs   Asia
    for a name   death   or mere difference
    came hurtling in improbable canoes
    heavy with liquor and fear
    bearing their beads and syphilis
    muzzleloaders and god

According to recent scientific theories, this
was the route taken by the earliest Indians,
at the end of the last Ice Age.

but from the truths that compel me
up the land's one nerve like a virus
to undo in a single day my father's lifetime
of westering
from my own lusts and neckties and novels
from ulcers   vitamins   bulletins   *accidia*
i lie unshielded under each motel's roof

Convenient to transcontinental railroads and a
four-lane hiway . . . offers American visitors every
modern . . . angler's paradise   big game . . .

under the uncontrollable cliffs and the starlight
falling on the same ice-bitten ranges
the first men saw

Having crossed from Asia to Alaska, and followed
the mammoths down corridors in the melting ice-cap,
these earliest Canadians are thought to have reached
a dead-end in their progress south, and been forced
to turn west from the Albertan plains into the Rockies
and so eventually came to the Pacific.

in that century the Siberians took   or more
(and took a hundred centuries ago)
to move by floes and hunger past the point
of no return   trailing the great woolly ones
    watching for the gleam of nine-foot tusks
    tracking   floundering in the newborn earth
    wolving by the black rivers that rattled
    from the glare of the narrowing icewalls
till the last red fountains
(*Mammuthus parelephas columbi*   his blood)
gushed on the boggy tundra
at the blind corridor's end

In the nearby museum, mounted specimens of
the wild life,

Surviving westward then over howling summits
the Siberians possessed these still fresh-hewn alps
(which i inheriting do not possess)
    They moved by day through bear and elk
    and by their killing
outliving sleep by capturing the deer's Wit
the Power of cougar
    in nets of dance and word
    the medicine of mask
    the threat of drum

and a spacious diorama outlining the story of
man. No charge.

Three mornings now from the applefoam
and the seas my Engine unreels me
out from the last gouged hills
like a bull straightens
into the prairie's arena
charges in a dazzle of snow the human mesh

Through Calgary, where the Blackfoot trail
once crossed, a four-lane artery helps speed
the traffic of Canada's greatest car-per-capita
city . . . in Bowness Park, life-sized models of
dinosaurs that once roamed the area

where all began for me
though the log cabin where first i was forced
into air
is a lost ghost under a vanished bridge
by a dying river

In 1912 Stampede Day was inaugurated to perpetuate
the finest traditions of the pioneer and cowpuncher . . .
now a week of parades, racing, rodeos, and other

An ash of ice whines at the cross of streets
A morning drunk is spattering curses
over a halfbreed girl in a blotched doorway

picturesque events . . . for the traveller from
the west, Calgary is the beginning of the
great Canadian prairie, which though largely
treeless, contains some of the world's richest
wheat-farms and oil deposits . . .

Far and far to the east again
i am pulled to a sky of land
flattened white to the Pole
i am drawn against the unstillable winds
    the breath of that madcap virgin
    mother of ice
    who embraced it all
    a wink ago in the world's eye
    till the sun won us again
    with his roving glance
    and sent her shrinking and weeping
    frozen lakes over the upstart grass

To the north, however, the rich postglacial
soil eventually gives place to tundra, perma-
frost and Arctic conditions . . .

Hoarding her cold passion she lies
the Greenland lodger
and the land's long face   and mine
cannot forget   is graved
with her monstrous rutting
Her time is our secret clock
She waits for all to slow
Then to lust back
wider than Europe and Pacific deep
    bringing her love   the rounded silence
        a long hard peace

Second coming
of the Ice Age ?

1965/1972

131

TO SWINDON FROM LONDON BY BRITRAIL
ALOUD/BAGATELLE

FF staccato	BOOOoooooottttt!
P lento Ped.	Brrrm brrbb brrrurn brrubb
poco a poco	brrrmbl brrubl brrrurnmble brumble
accel. e cresc.	brrrumble de bum brumble de *bug*
Ped. ad lib.	drumble le *dug* droomble de dag
MF stretto	drumbledee dug drumbledee dag
allegretto	droobedydag roobeddy dig
F	roobity bad rootilly bittle
rapido	roobity bag rubbity bottle
FF	brrrubeddidy rash crash crubberrydrubbery crosh
F molto rapido	croshoverrails Sroch hurry along
	hurryalong hurryalane hurryaloon hurryalung
	along alane along alung a-law-ing a-laying
MF allegro	adawdle alane a dawdel along
piu rall.	agoggle along a doggle de dung de
andante	*dawdillee doggillee goggillee gog*
MP tempo di valse	hungary dungaree mongrely dong
	mangletree anglesea mingle de BOOoooottt! Boot!
F——FFF brill.	hungary *dung* hunger me lung
F a tempo	ganger de lag gagger de lack gangerlag gagerlak
accel.	gangerlag gugelak lagaback loveaduck
	look at duck look at lake look at duck
MF vivace	lucky duck look at drake look at whooooosh!
accel.	izzza brisssss is a bridge!
F agitato	gurrrrdee *up* durridee *down* diddle de *grrp*
poco ritard.	de doodle de dup de diddle de dee BOOOOO!
con grazia——FF	de diddle de **BLAST** pasht pasht pasht pasht
energico presto	

cow & moos &——crash! clattr krradge——— & cows
crashes & ashes   & cows ashes & cow——WUNDRRR RR
RRRAILERER THUNder & ragerr blundrrrn gauge
gagelak gugelak   gagelak   gugelag
gagelllOOVer passOOver   passover pastdover
gagelak gugelak gagelak fugaluck
fugadug fulderol fuldedoodle   dedoodum
dedundr passundrrr   dedunderry boom
de bol de rol de boddle le dol
de puddle de pill   de roddle de rill
bottle a pole battle a post   buttery post
frettering peace feathering feast
pheasanty woods pleasanty words
clattering works blathering jerks
watery dirt dirtery what
waddery turds dirrery waw dirry whaw dirr whee
woof wee   whee with the trees withery twees
teas and trees an this an leaves an SQUOO! squaw!
gagelak gugelak gagerack pain pay in the train
bag baggity baggity kroom   baggy crude   ba koo
koo its a groom   doom an a fox   dog   fox
fox fox its a fox   dog dog dogelak grog
grogelak grief   grainalack grey
gag e lak   gud e lak   gug a KUNG...KUNG
guh   delhi   de   dung   de daddle   deee
SQUEEEEEEEEK K!——

The tren neow stendinnng on pletfoam thureee
is foh Suh——*weeeeen*——dawn.

dolce
PF agit.
FF strepitoso
molto agitato
F a tempo
FF subito con brio
MF rall.
a tempo

cantabile
ma non troppo
allegro assai

P calando
appassionato
espressivo
capriccio

PF legato sub. agit.
MF moderato
risoluto e rall.
ben marcato

MF grave
PF sostenuto
decresc.
FFF molto sost.

{ Con una certa
espressione
parlante

1965/1973

HOKKAI IN THE DEW LINE SNOWS

to sleep under real
stars   wake in the pupil of
original Sun

goodmornings with birds
love naked by waterfalls
o best planet—   whoooM!

a north door opens
the leaves scurry to hole &
the Cat prowls our world

Trumansburg, N.Y. 1966

after the calorestimated meal
in the male hall
they walk back to the compulibratories
keeping to the asphalt paths
conceived by the landtects

sometimes a thousand are in forward motion
engimechs the plureality   at 0826 hrs
in pairs   with crewcuts   hands by flanks
& slightly crooked below rainbreakers (yellow)
with *U of W* on back
ENGINEERS on upper sleeve L
& black number upper R

since none of this is actually required by deans
nor the gloves (black)   hushpuppies (gray)
nor absence of headcover & expression
what is felt is communiternity   a campustalt

the mathamen   cruts not quite so short
are sometimes grouped in 3s
but otherwise all waterloobed:
hands by flanks & slightly . . .(yellow) . . .
MATHS on . . .black . . .gray . . .absence
almost as striking — communalove at least

a few artsies yet (terminal class of '71)
midearburns / 1 in 10
dress as above of course
but some have briefcases in R hand
wear their ARTS upon their sleeves
& walk alone

1967

CHARITÉ, ESPÉRANCE ET FOI
(a tender tale from early ca-nada)

Once there were 3 little Indian girls
Champlain adopted them from the Montagnais
to show King Louis & the Cardinal it was possible
to make Christian Ladies out of savages
Faith He baptized them Foi (11) Espérance (12) et Charité (15)
Hope then put them in a fort to learn their French
Charity

Little Faith wriggled away & split for the woods
but Hope & Charity quickly mastered irregular verbs
& sewing   developed bosoms   went on to embroidery
When Champlain saw they had acquired piety & table manners
he dressed them in style & sailed downstream to Tadoussac
en route to the French Court with Espérance et Charité

But a wicked merchant named Nicholas Marsolet of Tadoussac
got Espérance aside & told her she was what he had to have
She said she had a date in France with King & God
Nick snarled he could have her & her sister given back
to the Indians   & grabbed her round her corset
She pulled a knife & got away to Charité

Les deux étudiantes then wrote Nicholas a letter
Hope began it:
     "Monsieur Marsolet, it was an honour & a pleasure to
     meet you, & I look forward to our next rencontre.
     In anticipation I have sharpened my knife so that
     I may on that occasion give myself the added joy
     of cutting out your heart"
& Charity added:
     "It will give me, monsieur, great pleasure
     to help my sister eat it."
All this sounded more elegant in the original of course
because that was in correct seventeenth-century French

They showed their letter to Champlain
He was impressed   no mistakes in tenses
He told them he was proud they had stood firm
especially against that méchant marchand Marsolet
who ate meat both Fridays & Saturdays   an Anglophile
& sold hooch to their cousin Indians in Tadoussac
However   Champlain added   he didnt think
that Espérance et Charité were ready yet for France

The two young ladies wept   unrolled their broderie
Champlain agreed they were bien civilisées
They went down on their knees   showed him their petticoats
Champlain was kind   admired the sewing   but was firm
It was France   he said   that wasnt ready yet for them
He gave them each a wooden rosary
& sent them back to Québec with Guillaume Couillard

Couillard was a respectable churchwarden & crop inspector
no merchant   he couldnt read & had 10 children of his own
He was the first to use the plough in Canada

but when Champlain got back from France nobody knew
where Hope & Charity had got to
or if they ever found their Faith again

Montréal 1967

CHAT bilingual

North Bay, Ontario 1967

SONG FOR SUNSETS

goodnite sun
im turning over again
im on the little ball
so slowly rolling
backwards from you

i hope youre there
central & responsible
burning away
all thru the black
of my dumb
somersault

i'll tumble around
& wake to you
the one who never sleeps
never notices
too busy keeping the whole
flock of us
rolling towards vega *brightest star in constellation Lyra*
without losing
our milky way

goodnite big dad
hasta la vista
hasta luego
we'll switch on now
our own small stars
& lie in darkness burning
turning
through unspace untime
& upsadaisy back
i trust to you

South Laguna, California 1968

A SMALL FACULTY STAG FOR THE VISITING POET

but a large quantity of brandy
                    on whisky
                    on sherry

At one table's end the Necessary Dean
has broken out cigars
At the other the Oxonian Canon
splotchfaced now
is putting us all down with naughty quotes
from Persius we're too slow to get
—except the Czech professor & the Hungarian
who dig everything
so civilised they're savage with disappointment
in us all & no doubt saying so this moment
safely across my chest in at least 2 languages

somewhere in the smoke the Librarian
is heard toasting the cummunwealth
& feck the Yenks
The Padre winces & gradually
like Yahweh in the Zohar withdraws his presence
leaving behind that vacuum of Evil
which is us

The Physics Department's chief cultural exhibit
also a very anthropological Native Son
have just asked me unanswerable questions
simultaneously from across the centrepiece

I am the dead eye of this verbal typhoon
I am the fraudulent word-doctor
stripped to dumbness by their tribal ritual
I am neither civilised nor savage but also Necessary

                    grinning
                    & stoned
                    & desolate

Australia 1968

MUSEUM OF MAN

the trustful curator has left me alone
in the closed wing of the aboriginal section

what's here?
3000 spears from arnhemland
waiting for a computer
to calculate their principle of balance

but what's in those wooden drawers?
i peek—sheeeez! shrunken heads
from new guinea
& dozens upon dozens
of twelve-inch penis sheaths

again
reference to penis

i'm going to lock doors
plant spears at windows
& try on everything for size

Adelaide 1968

CHRISTCHURCH, N.Z.

I have just flown 1100 miles from Australia
& landed in a Victorian bedroom
They sent up cindered muttonchops for lunch
There is an elderly reporter in my room with pince-nez
He wants to know why I have sideburns
& if I dont think being patronized by the Canada Council
isnt dangerous for my art or dont I feel I need to suffer?
In stone outside my window Capt. Scott
is nobly freezing to death near the South Pole
Suddenly I know the reporter is right
Sideburns have been sapping my strength

1968

cute.   *Easy way out.*

FOUR FEET BETWEEN
(for tony)

I was extending a patchwork of lint & batten
from ankle-sores to my new heel-cuts
absorbed in masochism & blessing my foresight
with bandaids   blessing too the voyagers
who brought breadfruit to Fiji
& this tree casting a benison of leaves
just where the volcano trail widens down
to the islet's only road
(though i'd conceded to myself
there were some million years of hindsight
before the breadfruit learned to grow
3-foot leaves & cannonball-sized seeds
to come to terms with perpetuity)
The cotton foliage on my purpling feet
argued however that i'd learned nothing much
from 60 years of being literate
nothing about coral poison anyway
or the agility of lava to mince mainland shoes

I was cosetting a raw big toe with my last band
when i grew conscious a slow pad of other feet
was on the trail   so close when i looked up
i caught myself in eyes deeplocked in a great face
Bula i said   trying to get it bass & guttural
His brows rose like wings   *Bula bula*! he said
quickly & stepped back
I must have got my hello close
& waited now for that wide Melanesian grin of welcome
But his stare was pitchy & the long bones of his face
seemed set in suspicion   even hostility
I could read nothing of him nor guess his age
the skin rough leather but the blast of hair
sootblack as any youth's
My height & about twice my width he stood there
a dark tree of flesh on the basalt stones

Suddenly he spoke   but in Fijian
i fumbled out my 7 words to say I couldnt speak it
He went back to staring   & i to my toepatch
Rooster-crows had been filtering thru the mangroves
There must be a village close   & he from it
I tried to forget it was near here only 90 years ago
these natives ate their last missionary
A bulbul began bulbuling in the breadfruit overhead
It stopped & there was only the far surf breathing
& the two of us

Mis-e-ter   yalo vinaka   He groped for English
police a wat you name a?   E-ro-la i said *what's yours?*
He muttered something cave-deep & gruff
no way i could repeat it   Should i try standing
& shaking hands?   But now his arms flew wide
and gestured at the road   *You wait a for bussy?*
Toot toot?   His eyes went back to my feet
I told him i'd just been swimming in the crater falls
was returning to the guesthouse in the port
He dug some of that perhaps   but threw out a big chest
made swimstrokes & waved at the lagoon   *Wy you no?*—
i filled in *Swim back by sea?*   & tried
against a steady wrinkling of sepia forehead
to tell him i'd been snorkeling all week
just for the fun but got rolled on the coral
& the port doctor warned me off reefs
till the sores healed but then today i'd—
But he'd lost me near the start   Brows furrowed
like walnuts he bent over me   mouth muscles agonized
to find the right sounds   *Yeara   ow mucha yeara you?*
Sixty-five i said & fingered it   For the first time
he smiled   *Me!* he nodded his tall pompom
me too   sickyfi'!

age in common

That spark had leaped the wordgulf   We were egged on
I learned he'd even heard of Canada   *far side a Hawaii*
though he'd been born in the rooster's village
My lord i thought   he's only one generation
from Cannibal King Thakembau   I began pulling on my sox
& asked him if he'd been as far as Suva
His busby shook   *Sa sega   No alla tima here*
He looked more proud than sad
With a mahogany finger then he made an airy circle
You? You go rowna worela? Io i said *Yes*
& felt ashamed   He turned as if satisfied
but swung back & flung out at last the real question
E-ro-la   watta wrong a you feet?

I tried again & got nowhere   This wasnt tourist country
He'd never met a fullgrown man who went up the volcano
without a boar-spear   & swam in cold waterfalls
& dived in the sea only to be looking
But most of all he couldnt understand what hurt my feet
And so he stood   a statue of Melanic Power
maroon cheeks under a storm of hair
torso cicatriced with the darker scars of tribal rites
endured a half-century ago   a skirt of sorrel reeds
& all mounted on two unfeeling pedestals of meat
two tough sun-barbecued planksteaks of feet
like those his cousins use   across the bay on Benga
to walk on white-hot stones   for magic or for tourists

What's wrong my feet i said *is I not born here too*
He laughed   the only time   with a solid flash of teeth
Bussy come a some a time he said gently *you be o rite*
Ni sa mothe Goobye   He went paddling swiftly up the trail
You o-rite now i called   & lay back to wait the bus
under the breadfruit tree

Levuka 1969

ON THE NIGHT JET

small waffle-irons glowing
on a huge farmhouse stove
crossroad towns of the prairies
seven miles below

faint rods of highways
electroscopic genes

mainly only the stars
of the farms
lonely as the others
like reflections above
(below?)
and as remote
from me
now
on the night
jet

Over Saskatchewan 1970

40 ft of wing out there
suddenly i want to walk
into that sun
but capt loudspeaker says
headwinds 105 mph speed another 400
at once im walking back on air

    !BUT WHAT A FUN DEATH!

                          alt 35000
                    nothing but
            7
            miles of
high dive
at last i can practice   k
     g   c   n
   a   a   i
       i   j   f
                                    e
 r s   n   s
       e
                    o a r
              b   d
 s p r i n g   i
                            n
                            g
down
     from   c l o u d
                     to   c l o u d

(o yes acceleration 32 ft per sec per sec)
but ive 7 m to play with
& all that wind d r i f t
& b o d yf l a P

ive got time at last to break the world
's record for b (i once dreamed about)   s^om
      a   e
      c   r
      k   s
               a$_u$ l$_t$

before straightening into a   s
        AA
        SS
       WW
        AA
 N_NN_{NN}N^NN
      Ɐ

so widearmed & precise i am

embracing   s e e e !

the whole world & time
in one last sweet tick of li—

but no one lets me walk out
too hard to break this doubleglass
i'll have to be content again
with the usual smooth landing
dead on
& the meek shuffle into the pens
to wait my turn somewhere
at ground level
under the overcast ahead.

Edmonton, Alberta 1969

FROM THE BRIDGE: FIRTH OF FORTH

blood veins
of the flowering gorse
run down
to the blind waters

terns
dive on the islets
and salt the ruins
of castles
built in the second world war

under the butterflies
of yachts
how long the shadow
of the nuclear submarine

En route to Aberdeen 1971

CANADA: CASE HISTORY: 1973

No more the highschool land
deadset in loutishness
This cat's turned cool
the gangling's gone
guffaws are for the peasants

Inside his plastic igloo now
he watches gooks and yankees bleed
in colour on the telly
But under a faded Carnaby shirt
ulcers knife the rounding belly

Hung up on rye and nicotine and sex-
y flicks, kept off the snow and grass
he teeters tiptoe on his arctic roof
(ten brittle legs, no two together)
baring his royal canadian ass
white and helpless in the global winds

Schizoid from birth, and still a sado-masochist
this turkey thinks that for his sins
he should be carved while still alive:
legs to Québec, the future Vietnam;
the rest, self-served and pre-digested,
to make a Harvest Home for Uncle Sam. . . .

Teeth shot and memory going
(except for childhood grudges),
one moment murderous, the next depressed,
this youth, we fear, has moved from adolescence
into what looks like permanent senescence.

Toronto

NO BODY
(coming home from the airport)

i walk home in snow-slush
plodding alone imagining
the leap of pulse
under your graywool glove

snow slants down
an endless flock
of tiny bird-flakes
over me they wheel
and for a while move upward
having nowhere to fall
since you went away

the flat's not real
like a room "restored"
in a Pioneer Museum
exact but unconvincing
where is the being
who gave the armchair meaning?
i do not think
the TV will turn on

your small slippers
wait by the chesterfield
they do not move
something arranged
by a slick director
they lack the feet
which are human and complete
with minuscule calluses

i water the yellow chrysanthemum
silent as a photograph
nothing drinks
the armchair
stiff with air

only the bed grows
and is heard
it is twice as big already
and noisily empty
and yet an imitation too
a stuffed animal
nothing warm under the fur
no
body

Alexander Street, Toronto 1973

SHE IS
(for wai-lan, on her 24th birthday)

she is
a little spruce tree
fresh & every way
herself
like a dawn

when warm winds come
she will move
all her body
in a tremble of light

but today she stands
in magical stillness
she has clasped
all my falling flakes
from the round of her sky
and wished them
into her own
snowtree

through the cold time
she holds me
with evergreen
devotion
she bears up my whiteness

o so light may i press
letting each needle
grow in her own
symmetry

for i am at peace
in her form
after whirling
and faithful to all
her curves

but when warm winds come
we must stir from this trance
she will lift living arms
to the sun's dance

i will slide then
in a soft caress
of her brown sides
and my falling will end
somewhere in her roots

may my waters then
bring her strength only
help her hold trim
and evergreen her being
with suns and winds
for o many and many
and happiest years

Treehouse, Uxbridge 1974

BESTIARY

- resembling a beast
- lacking intelligence or reason

an arkfull she is
of undulant creatures
a cinnamon bearcub
curled in a warm ball
thinking of honey & berries
nuts roots or even
grass jelly for supper

a sturdy raccoon too
with masked eyes
& dexterous forepaws
very frequent to bathe
& a bandit of ice cream
who sleeps a lot
with one soft hindpaw
poking most modestly out

or a shy bobcat
coloured olivebrown
or maybe pale gold
with round
slipper-fur feet
on which she sits very quiet
and so thoughtful
beside her leafy plants
she is sometimes invisible
though very much there

she can be an ochre
squirrel as well
sinuous & all compact
alert & frisky
& away & back like a dream

whatever creature
she is its peaceful emissary
most faithful
most loving

Toronto 1974

154

ON HER TWENTY-SIXTH BIRTHDAY

At six you folded paper boats
with nowhere to sail them down
except a tub in chinatown

Sixteen you climbed into a dory
to heave through sloughs of English Lit.
and came by a dying lake to sit

Then we shaped our own canoe
birch-delicate but strong
and big enough for two

Over the portage freed
we steer through rapids worth the battling
They flow to a living sea

Sit straight dear twenty-six
hold firm the blade you've made
Mine dips with yours however frayed

With luck and will we'll reach
at last some bronzed arbutus beach
From there you'll sail the world

Give my old paddle then a simple burning
Sift the ashes down
where fish and weed are turning

    But today   sweet twenty-six
    rest your eyes from the current's shine
    loose your small palms from the coursing
    let them find mine

Balliol St., Toronto 27 January 1976

Index of Titles

OTHER BOOKS BY EARLE BIRNEY

Published by McClelland & Stewart, Toronto, Ont.
   Collected Poems, 2 vols., 1975, $20.
   Damnation of Vancouver, a play, 1977, $1.95.
   Down the long table (fiction), New Canadian Library, 1975,
      $2.95.
   Turvey, a military picaresque, unexpurgated, ed., 1976, $8.95;
      New Canadian Library, paper, $2.95.

Obtainable from the author, 2201/200 Balliol St., Toronto, Ont.
   The cow jumped over the moon/the writing & reading of poetry,
      1972, $3.

obsessed by lusty women
57
p.64 mes. women
100 lust

Man destroys nature 76

Human p.81, 83
- full of stench of human indignity p.116
- dwells on human indifference in our vast world.